Praise for *If God Is For Us*

If the Bible were a mountain range, it is said, Romans 8 would be its highest peak. I can say after reading this study that Trillia Newbell is a sure-footed mountain guide that will help you climb this great passage and get some of its best breathtaking views of God and our salvation in Christ. I highly recommend this volume!

TIM KELLER, cofounder, Redeemer City to City

So often we encounter the message of Romans 8 in fragments, its best-known verses lifted from their context and lightly quoted to suit the need of the moment. With a careful hand, Trillia Newbell mends our fragmented reading by guiding us into the text, orienting this crucial chapter within the book of Romans as a whole, and tracing its cohesive message from start to finish. *If God Is For Us* is six weeks well spent for any earnest student of the Bible.

JEN WILKIN, author and Bible teacher

Trillia Newbell is a gift to the church. I can think of few people whose lives more authentically display the work of God and the fruit of His Spirit. This study on the eighth chapter of Romans will bless, encourage, and challenge you to grow further into Christ. Within these pages, Trillia serves as a faithful guide to help you better understand and apply God's Word to your life.

RUSSELL MOORE, President, The Ethics & Religious Liberty Commission of the Southern Baptist Convention

Like a delicious meal, Romans 8 is packed with truths to be savored as they are slowly enjoyed. *If God Is For Us* helps us to slow down and ponder the riches in this beloved chapter line by line, one verse at a time. Trillia Newbell's warmth and wisdom will guide and encourage you with truths that will refresh and revive your soul.

MELISSA KRUGER, director of women's content for The Gospel Coalition and author of *In All Things*

Some in the church eschew discipleship and study because they "don't have time" or "don't know how." Written like a letter from a good friend, *If God Is For Us* offers a deep and digestible look into Paul's intimate writings in Romans 8. Trillia explores in detail the radical, existential transformation made possible through Christ. If you've hesitated on Romans because it seems overwhelming, *If God Is For Us is* an excellent doorway to understanding, living, and sharing the "exchanged life."

K. A. ELLIS, Cannada Fellow for World Christianity at Reformed Theological Seminary

I'm so thankful for Trillia and this thorough study on Romans 8. Trillia does a beautiful job encouraging us to be in God's Word without leaving us to do it alone. Her insights and personal illustrations make studying this foundational chapter of Scripture accessible and inviting. I encourage you to get a group of friends together and pick up a copy of *If God Is For Us.*

KELLY MINTER, Bible teacher and author of *No Other Gods*

If God Is For Us is an extraordinary study and one I wholeheartedly recommend. I have read and studied Romans 8 at length, as it is one of my favorite chapters in the Bible, and God has used it to free me and transform me. And yet, through this six-week study with Trillia, God opened the eyes of my heart anew to the beauty of the gospel, and deepened my gratitude for the unwavering love of our Father and the gift of His precious Son, Jesus.

JEANNIE CUNNION, author of *Mom Set Free*

Trillia Newbell's passion for God's Word leaps off each page of this exceptional 6-week study. Wisely, she sweeps through the early chapters of Romans first, preparing our hearts for a deeply satisfying walk through Romans 8, verse by powerful verse. Her scholarship is impressive, and her questions are probing. Above all, her honest confessions and personal discoveries bring home the life-altering truths contained in this beloved chapter of the Bible. A wonderful resource!

LIZ CURTIS HIGGS, bestselling author of *Bad Girls of the Bible*

Trillia Newbell's *If God Is For Us* is an insightful, accessible, and in-depth study of one of the Bible's most treasured chapters. It offers a fresh and practical Bible study methodology that inspires the reader to want more. In a season when women are searching for strong theological representation and quality biblically based resources, Trillia has certainly delivered.

MISSIE BRANCH, Asst. Dean of Students to Women, Southeastern Baptist Theological Seminary

Trillia's study encourages us to mine for deep treasure in one of the most gospel-rich chapters of the Bible, as she seamlessly shifts between deep inductive study and thoughtful devotional reading. This curriculum will be a blessing to many!

EMILY JENSEN and LAURA WIFLER, cofounders of Risen Motherhood

Depending on your relationship with Scripture, studying a chapter for an entire month can seem boring, but this study guide highlights the importance of patient study over broad study. Yet, its focused style is far from intimidating to those who have an avoidant posture toward learning. Trillia Newbell offers a highly accessible and introspective study into Romans 8, which rightfully seeks to lead us to the main elements of the text and also gives us a chance to see ourselves more clearly. In this study, we see the faithfulness of God, the grace offered in repentance, and the reality of suffering for Christ's sake, if we are in the Lord. Newbell reminds us that, "Because we are Christ's, we keep on fighting sin, knowing that grace is available when we fail."

CHRISTINA H. EDMONDSON, Dean for Intercultural Student Development at Calvin College

It's easy to think that believers are somehow immune to the shackles that once bound our souls. The truth is, like the Israelites who questioned God's goodness in the desert, quickly forgetting how awful slavery really was, we sometimes slip into believing that maybe God isn't really for us. In our pain, our confusion, our flat-out tiredness, our Bibles gather dust and our half-hearted prayers get drowned out in the lure "of just one more episode" or "only five more minutes of scrolling." Two hours later, we are still tired and maybe even a little jaded that life has become a series of *just getting through the days*, hoping for something to give us the spark we once had. Of course, we wouldn't dare say these things out loud. The truth is, under the surface of things, we're desperate for revival. We could all use some resurrection, some life out of the daily deadness we so often feel. In *If God Is For Us*, Trillia Newbell takes us into Romans 8 and asks us to let God remind us of who He is, who we are to Him, and where life is found and hope is more than a trite offering. If you're in a season where life feels like it just keeps coming against you, like you can't get a break, *If God Is For Us* is the study your soul is longing for.

SARAH MAE, author of *The Complicated Heart*

IF GOD

THE *Everlasting* TRUTH
OF OUR GREAT *Salvation*

IS

FOR US

A 6-WEEK
BIBLE STUDY OF
Romans 8

TRILLIA J. NEWBELL

MOODY PUBLISHERS

CHICAGO

We hope you enjoy this book from Moody Publishers. Our goal is to provide high-quality, thought-provoking books and products that connect truth to your real needs and challenges. For more information on other books and products written and produced from a biblical perspective, go to www.moodypublishers.com or write to:

Moody Publishers
820 N. LaSalle Boulevard
Chicago, IL 60610

1 3 5 7 9 10 8 6 4 2

Printed in the United States of America

To my dearest daughter, Sydney:
May the Lord make the truth in these pages
grow deep in your heart
and may you be an instrument He uses
to spread it like wildfire.
For His glory.
Because of His grace.

CONTENTS

ABOUT THIS STUDY

Blessed is the man . . .
[whose] delight is in the law of the Lord,
> and on his law he meditates day and night.
Psalm 1:1–2

I have stored up your word in my heart,
> that I might not sin against you.
Psalm 119:11

Are you a pendulum swinger? Most of us are. We get an idea about one thing, the idea is corrected or adjusted, and then we swing all the way in the opposite direction. This happens in many areas of life, including how we approach reading our Bibles.

Perhaps you grew up thinking that the only way to approach the Word of God was to read a verse (or verses, or chapter) every morning. Or maybe you were told that the only way to truly understand the Word is to use a commentary or other study aid along with your Bible reading. Maybe you've adopted the idea that the only way to read the Word is to do an inductive Bible study. Or perhaps you have given up any organized approach altogether—you simply don't know what to do!

I'm here to encourage you that there is freedom in how you approach God's Word. There are, of course, best practices for understanding the Word, ones we will explore further below. But the important thing is to *do* it, to spend some quality time with God's living and active words about Himself and the supremacy of His

Son. My primary goal in this study is to make it a little easier for you to do that. It may challenge you if you are new to Bible study, but it will be well worth it in the end. That is my hope and prayer for you!

My hope is that what we do here will give you some creative ideas for different ways to learn about our awesome God, His glorious Son, and His amazing Spirit while enjoying this gift of God's words for you and me (2 Tim. 3:16–17). I also hope it will give you some new insights into the letter from Paul that many consider his most powerful and, more specifically, the pivotal part of that letter that we know as Romans 8. My hope is that you will learn to and enjoy studying deeply, meditating often, and responding when prompted by the Spirit to what you read.

WHAT THIS STUDY OFFERS

This six-week study is unique in that it is a hybrid—a Bible study and devotional combined. Each week will include the following:

- An introduction to the week's study.

- Daily or weekly "Read" prompts to get you into the Word. Beginning in week two, there will also be some suggestions for enriching your reading by approaching the readings in a variety of ways.

- "Respond" questions to help you dig into what you've read and understand it better.

- Five days' worth of "Explore" devotionals to support you in thinking about the text and applying it to your life.

- Five days' worth of "Reflect" questions to give you more to think and pray about.

Note that the first week of the study is structured a little differently than the ones that follow. It features daily Bible readings and "Respond" questions based on those readings as it takes you through the seven chapters of Romans that lead to chapter 8. There is also a devotional for each day (five days a week) plus a set of "Reflect" questions to help you meditate on what you've read.

After that first week, though, as we dive into Romans 8, we'll shift gears a little. There will be only one reading and one set of "Respond" questions for the entire week, but there will still be daily "Consider" devotionals, daily "Reflect" questions, and daily suggestions for meditating on the weekly reading.

MAKE IT WORK FOR YOU!

I encourage you to take advantage of the flexibility built into this study to make it work for you. It's designed to be done in a group setting or individually. Here are just a few of the possibilities.

- Do the study entirely on your own at home.

- Meet daily with a few friends in-person (maybe for coffee) or online to share your response to the devotionals and the questions.

- Try a combination—do some of it (like the devotionals) at home and some of it (like selected study or reflection questions) in a weekly group gathering. Or study at home and then come together to discuss your insights and discoveries.

You can follow the suggested pattern of five days of study, two days off, or you can stretch out the material to cover six or even seven days. Personally I like the idea of reading and study on one day, devotionals and reflections on five more days, and then taking a "sabbath" day of rest.

SOME BIBLE STUDY BASICS

Are you new to studying the Bible? Here are a few tips to help you get started. (These steps apply to studying any part of the Bible.)

Step #1: Read the Passage Straight Through in One Sitting

The Bible is the inspired Word of God (1 Cor. 2:12–13, 2 Tim. 3:16–17), but it is also a book! Therefore, I encourage you to begin your study of any part of the Bible by simply reading it that way—like a book. Feel free to write down certain themes you see, repeated words, and key terms, but don't get bogged down in the details at first.

For the purposes of this study, in fact, I suggest that you begin by reading the entire book of Romans straight through. This will give you a sweeping overview of this powerful letter, which certainly wasn't divided into chapters and verses when Paul sent it to the Christians in Rome. Although we will spend the bulk of our time in chapter 8, knowing what is going on elsewhere in Romans will provide a helpful perspective.

Step #2: Clarify the Context

Have you ever walked up to some friends talking or overheard a conversation that seemed off or even inappropriate? I have. Once I walked up to a conversation already in progress and heard a woman say she had thrown a cat out of a window. I was confused and upset. But I quickly discovered that in context her statement made sense. She had thrown a stuffed toy out of a window and down to a little girl.

Knowing the context of that conversation helped me a lot—and clarifying context helps us understand Scripture as well. In this study we will spend a little extra time on the context of Romans 8 because many of us haven't been taught to think about the context of Scripture. So we often go straight to the application without fully understanding the text itself.

What kind of context are we looking for when it comes to Bible study? For any book or passage, we need to consider:

- Who wrote it?

- When was it written?

- Who was it written for (the audience)?

- Why was it written (its purpose)?

- What was going on with God's people and the world in general when it was written?

- How does it relate to other parts of God's Word?

If you don't know the answers to any of these context questions, the section below on finding help will show you some good places to look.

Step #3: Consider What the Passage Says—and What It Means

Once you have done those early steps, it's time to look for the meaning. What is the actual sense of the text, and what is it saying to you? Often the meaning is clear, but sometimes you may need to reread, ponder, and maybe even look up the words before you have a clear sense of what it is saying. (Many of the "Respond" questions in this book are designed to help you do just that.)

This is a great time for cross-referencing, which is mentioned in our study of Romans 8. Cross-referencing, as the name implies, simply means comparing the passage you are studying to other passages in the Bible that can help you understand the meaning of the text. Looking at the text surrounding the verse you are reading also helps with both context and interpretation.

I always find it helpful to look for the gospel in the text—how it relates to Jesus and His saving work in the world. (Since the whole of God's story points to Jesus, you can do this even with Old Testament texts.)

Step #4: Apply the Text to Your Life

The Bible's message is meant to be lived as well as read, so look closely for what God is telling you through His Word. Sometimes the application will practically leap out on the page. Other times, you might have to live with the text, reflect on it, and pray about it. That's okay. The more time you spend in the Word, relying on the Holy Spirit, the more you'll find yourself turning to it for guidance.

NEED HELP?

As you read through the book of Romans and attempt to answer the questions in this study, you may find yourself struggling at times, especially if you are new to Romans and to Bible study in general. The apostle Paul's writing is rich in meaning, but it can also be complex. You might also discover you need a little more background or explanation about Paul's references, the meaning of certain words, or how the concepts in Romans 8 compare to other parts of Romans or the Bible in general. Or you might simply want to dig deeper into the text, as many of the study questions in this book encourage you to do.

Where do you go for help? Start with your own Bible! Chances are it contains most of what you need to understand what you are reading. Many Bibles include a concordance or cross-references (to direct you to other places in the Bible where a particular idea can be found), background notes, even commentaries.

If your Bible doesn't have these aids—or if you want more help—a wealth of other resources is readily available, and you don't have to spend a lot of money and time to make use of them. Here are a few possibilities:

- *Other versions of the Bible.* I primarily use the English Standard Version, which gives a very accurate word-for-word translation of Paul's original Greek, and I have used this translation as a basis for this study. Many of the "Respond" questions refer directly to the wording of the ESV, so you may have an easier time with them if you also use it. But you may find some other versions helpful as a supplement, and of course the ESV is not a requirement. Biblegateway.com and biblehub.com are two online sites that put different translations and paraphrases at your fingertips.

- *Study aids.* You don't have to buy a library of commentaries, Bible dictionaries, lexicons, and such to find some help. If your church has a library, look there for these aids. You can find excellent help at biblegateway.com, biblehub.com (my favorite!), and several other sites.

- *Other resources.* In the back of this book you'll find a list of books, videos, and other resources I've consulted while preparing this study. I recommend them for further exploration.

- *Other Christians!* If you're doing this study as a group, you'll be able to compare notes with other group members. But even if you're doing it on your own, seek out opportunities to ask questions or compare notes with others. You will benefit from the unique perspective of others.

However you choose to approach this study, I hope you will find it enriching and inspiring—six weeks that draw you closer to Christ and give you a deeper and more grateful appreciation for His gospel.

INTRODUCTION

A CHERISHED BOOK, A FAVORITE CHAPTER

If someone had come up to me on the morning of my wedding day and asked me if I knew my husband-to-be well, I would have said yes without hesitation. Now, fifteen years later, I realize that while I did know him before I married him, I know so much more about him now. Our relationship has deepened, and my knowledge of him has exponentially increased since our wedding.

Why? Because we've spent hours upon hours together. We know each other's history. We know our backgrounds. When one of us reacts to something, the other knows the context from which the reaction comes. We know each other because we have studied, learned, enjoyed, and listened to each other over the course of these many years. And I'm looking forward to learning even more in the years to come!

It takes time to really know a person—and the same thing is true about getting to know the Bible. After nearly twenty years of "living with" the Bible and many, many hours of study, I'm only beginning to scratch the surface of its rich depths. And even with all my studying, I realize I will never exhaust the potential depths of learning about the Lord.

Does that sound a little daunting? It does to some people. As a matter of fact, some may avoid coming to the Word because they fear misinterpreting it. Others may only pick out a few of their favorite verses and never learn anything else. But

I don't want that for you. I encourage you to just dive in, because every step in developing a relationship has value, even the simplest "getting to know you" ones.

Before we dive into Romans 8, therefore, let's get to know the book a little. We will only scratch the surface, but that surface knowledge will help us as we study Romans 8. Just as in a marriage, our understanding and love for the Word will only grow as we learn more about it. I imagine that as we spend time in God's Word together, learning more about the writers, intent, context, and background, we will only desire to learn more about the next biblical book we read. So let's dive in.

The book of Romans was written by the apostle Paul to the churches in Rome. Most scholars agree that he likely wrote the letter while spending three months in the city of Corinth (see Acts 20:2–3). Although Paul was a Jew, he wrote the letter in Greek, a language understood in those days by Jews and Gentiles alike. And, as with most of his letters to churches, this letter addresses issues that would concern the particular church it was addressed to.

Although the exact or main purpose of Romans has been debated,[1] most scholars agree that the gospel and the glory of God are central themes. Paul proclaimed, "For I am not ashamed of the gospel, for it is the power of God for salvation to everyone who believes, to the Jew first and also to the Greek" (Rom. 1:16). And he had a desire to "preach the gospel" to those in Rome (Rom. 1:15).

This is easy to see when you actually get into the text because the gospel practically pours out of its pages—so much so that Christians have often used the book as a tool for evangelism. Perhaps you've heard of the "Romans Road," for instance. It's a method of using certain verses in Romans (3:23, 3:10–18, 5:8, 6:23, 10:8, and so forth) as a guide for sharing the gospel with someone who needs to hear it.[2]

1. Some believe that there was conflict between Jewish Christians and Gentile Christians in the Roman church. And it is true that throughout the book of Romans we see Paul addressing Jew-and-Gentile issues—from explaining the function of the law (Rom. 1–3, 5:20, and 7:1–25) to Abraham's relationship to the Gentile Christians (4:1–25). The likelihood of conflict between these two groups in Rome would also be consistent with what we read in other New Testament books such as Acts, Galatians, and Ephesians.
2. For a simple explanation of this tool, see "What Is the Romans Road to Salvation?," Got Questions, https://www.gotquestions.org/Romans-road-salvation.html.

We should pause here to recognize something important, however. Paul wrote this letter to the church in Rome, which means he was not speaking of preaching the gospel to unbelievers, but rather to his fellow Christians. From this we can deduce that the truth and implications of the gospel apply to all of the Christian life. In other words, you and I need to hear the gospel too—daily.

Also, keep in mind that the Christians at this time would have experienced persecution for their faith. So verses like Romans 8:36—which speaks of being killed for Jesus' sake—would not only have been meaningful, but literally true! To not be ashamed of the gospel in those days could have been a death sentence. But as Paul reminded the Christians in Rome—and you and me as well—our suffering doesn't compare to the glory that will eventually be revealed to us (Rom. 8:18).

This message is one that has resonated with Christians throughout the centuries and has changed many lives. Even today, if you ask believers for their favorite book of the Bible, many would place Romans at the top of the list. And if you were to take a survey and ask what specific chapter in the Bible has had the most impact on their lives, a number would name the eighth chapter of Romans—and for good reason.

Tim Keller has written that "the book of Romans is the most sustained explanation of the heart of the gospel, and the most thrilling exploration of how that gospel goes to work in our hearts."[3] I agree wholeheartedly. And to me, Romans 8 is the heart of that great letter. It provides the assurance of this great salvation, summed up in its first compelling sentence, which proclaims to its reader that there is no condemnation in Christ Jesus (8:1).

That amazing declaration would be enough, but there's more, so much more. We learn throughout Romans 8 that:

- The Spirit is actively at work in us (8:4–11);

---

3. Tim Keller, *Romans 8–16 for You*, God's Word for You Romans Series, Book 2 (London, UK: Good Book Company, 2014), 7.

- We are heirs with Christ, the adopted children of God (8:12–17);

- Our suffering is for a great purpose and doesn't compare to the glory we will experience (8:18–25);

- Even in our weakness, the Spirit is at work (8:26–27);

- God is working all things for our good (8:28);

- And absolutely nothing can ever separate us from the love of Christ (8:31–39).

Need I go on? Oh, I can, and I want to! I haven't even gotten to the five life-changing questions that solidify our conviction that God is absolutely, undeniably for us (8:31–38).

So in case you've been concerned whether a single chapter in a single book can sustain an entire six-week study, don't worry. We could probably spend another six weeks—or a lifetime—and still find more.

If God Is For Us will take us on a journey into Romans 8, reminding us of our great salvation, our inheritance, and ultimately the love of our good Father. Romans 8 can be easily quoted—and often is—but through *If God Is For Us* I hope that we might meditate deeply on it, soaking in the goodness of this truth and rejoicing in the mind-boggling reality that God intends nothing but good for us. My prayer is that, together, we'll gain a greater understanding of the significance of this passage of Scripture and why these verses mean so much to so many.

We will accomplish this through reading the text, through studying God's Word, through daily reflection on the passages, and ultimately through prayer. But God must do the work in our hearts for us to understand. Let's ask God to help us as we seek to know the God of our salvation in ever-deepening ways.

no greater message

The goal of week one is to get an overview of Romans and read through its first seven chapters. Although our study focuses primarily on Romans 8, it is good to have a general understanding of what comes before it. Chapter 8 of Romans begins with the word *therefore,* which means that everything that comes before it is important and connected.

Much of this week, *therefore,* involves reading and responding to Romans 1–7. There will be content questions to work through each day as well as a daily devotional and more questions for reflection.

If this seems like a lot of reading and questions, don't worry. Once we get into Romans 8, there will be a lot less reading and more in-depth reflection. In the meantime, don't fret if some of your reading runs over into a sixth day or a seventh or if you don't get through all the questions. Just get through it all the best you can. (If you're working on your own, you might even consider taking an extra week for this first step.) I guarantee it will be worth it in the long run.

WEEK ONE | DAY ONE

Remember, this initial week is a sweep through the first seven chapters of Romans. Feel free to read and study further into one chapter or another, stick with and cross reference one key verse, or simply spend time working to gain a broader understanding of each day's text.

READ | ROMANS 1–2

RESPOND

1. Who wrote the book of Romans? When was it written, and to whom was it written?

2. How would you summarize Romans 1? Why does Paul say he is not ashamed of the gospel, and what might that mean for the rest of the book?

3. What does Romans 1:18–32 say about the human condition—what people are like and what it's like to live in this world? What do these verses say about God? And what might they say about you specifically?

4. Why do you think Paul repeats the phrase translated "O man" in the ESV translation of 2:1–3? How do other versions translate these verses? (Note: there is repetition in the original Greek too.)

5. Why do you think Paul mentions the Jews and Greeks in reference to both the gospel (1:16) as well as in the wrath to come (2:10)? Why might Paul repeat the "Jews come first" idea for each?

6. The word *law* is mentioned several times in 2:12–29. In verse 12, when Paul refers to those "in the law" and those "outside of the law" he is referring to Jews (the people of Israel or covenant people) as opposed to the Gentiles (those who were not Jews). Look up 1 Corinthians 9:20–22, where Paul explains how he "became a Jew" to win Jews and "became as one outside the law" in order to win Gentiles. With some of this context in mind, review the references to the *law* in Romans 2:12–29. What are some of the implications you see in this text concerning the law?

7. Circumcision is mentioned several times in our text (2:25–29). It also appears throughout the Old Testament, beginning in Genesis 17. According to that Genesis passage, what did circumcision mean for the Jewish people? With that in mind, why do you think circumcision was an issue for the early Christians? Why might Paul's statement in Romans 2:25 be alarming to his Jewish readers? How is he ultimately pointing to the need of an ultimate sacrifice?

8.   What do you think this line from 2:29 means: "But a Jew is one inwardly, and circumcision is a matter of the heart, by the Spirit, not by the letter. His praise is not from man but from God"?

EXPLORE

Not Ashamed

I am not ashamed of the gospel, for it is the power of God for salvation to everyone who believes, to the Jew first and also to the Greek. For in it the righteousness of God is revealed from faith for faith, as it is written, "The righteous shall live by faith."
ROMANS 1:16–17

I sat across from my friend, spilling my guts. I couldn't wait to share with her because I was so desperate for help.

As she sat there listening to me share my sorrows, I could tell she was carrying my burden. Her eyebrows buckled, and her eyes welled up with tears. She really wanted to take away my pain. But she was wise enough to know that I needed more than comfort or sympathy or even her advice. What I needed was a Person—Jesus. My sin separated me from God, and the only remedy for that was the saving work of Jesus on the cross.

My friend had many reasons why she could have finished our conversation that day without sharing the gospel with me. I was older than she was and came from a different background. We were really just friendly acquaintances, not great friends. But none of these reasons mattered to her. Why? Because she was not ashamed of the gospel or afraid to share it.

Paul had even greater reason to worry about sharing the gospel than my friend did. He was well aware of the violent persecution associated with such efforts in those days—after all, he had been a persecutor! But Paul, too, was neither ashamed of the gospel nor afraid to share it.

Perhaps this is because both my friend and Paul knew the power of the gospel to transform lives—their own first and foremost. Their transformation stories are quite different. My friend was saved at a very young age. Paul had perhaps the most dramatic conversion in all of history—a bright light on a dark road, the voice of Jesus, being literally blinded so he could see the truth. Both, however, experienced a radical transformation—literally from death to life. And I did, too, because of my friend's willingness to share the gospel with me.

You don't need to have a radical testimony like Paul's to know the power of the gospel to change lives. What you and I need is the faith to believe. There will come a time, if the time hasn't already come, when we will have the choice to either proclaim Jesus or shrink back and say nothing. We might feel inadequate or be tempted to second-guess ourselves. Or we might find the thought of rejection too much to bear. But if we believe the gospel to be true—that God sent His only Son, Jesus, who was fully God and fully man; that Jesus lived a perfect life on earth, died on the cross, and then rose and defeated death; that Jesus is the way (the *only* way), the truth, and the life—then isn't it selfish for us to keep this incredibly good, radically transformational news to ourselves?

You and I can repent of our fear and complacency, knowing that God is rich in grace and mercy, and ask the Lord to give us faith—not in our power or perfect words, but rather in the power of the gospel to save.

REFLECT

1.   Take a moment to reflect on your personal testimony. When and how did you become a Christian?

2.   Can you say with confidence, "I'm not ashamed of the gospel"? If so, why? If not, what's making you ashamed or uncertain?

3.   Think of people in your life—maybe friends or family—with whom you've been hoping to share the gospel but haven't yet done so. What has held you back?

4.   Take a moment to pray for the opportunities and boldness to share the gospel and for the Lord to work in the lives of those who will hear you share.

WEEK ONE | DAY TWO

READ | ROMANS 3–4

RESPOND

1. Why do you think Paul focuses on the faith of the Jews in chapter 3:1–4?

2. What does it mean to be "under the power of sin" (see 3:9–10)?

3. According to Paul, what does the law do for us in regard to sin (3:20)? What does it *not* do?

4. The words *righteous* and *righteousness* appear multiple times in 3:1–26. (How many times will depend on what version of the Bible you are using.) What do these words mean, and what do they tell us about God? About ourselves?

5. We also see the words *justified*, *just*, and *justifier* in the 3:1–26 passage. What do those words mean? How are they applied to both the Jew and Gentile by faith? What do these words tell us about God?

6. Paul writes in 4:1–2 that even Abraham can't boast. Why can't he, and why can't we?

7. Read Genesis 17:9–14 again to understand the origin of circumcision and what it meant to the Jews. Read Leviticus 12:2–3 to see how circumcision was also a part of the Mosaic law. According to Paul in Romans 4, what was the purpose of circumcision in regard to justification and faith? How was this explanation significant to his first-century readers? Why is this significant for us today?

8. So much good news is contained in the phrase "counted to us" (4:23–25). What does this phrase mean? Why is it such good news?

EXPLORE

Unfaithful

What if some were unfaithful? Does their faithlessness nullify the faithfulness of God? By no means! Let God be true though every one were a liar, as it is written,

*"That you may be justified in your words,
and prevail when you are judged."*

*But if our unrighteousness serves to show the righteousness of God, what
shall we say? That God is unrighteous to inflict wrath on us? (I speak in a
human way.) By no means! For then how could God judge the world?*
ROMANS 3:3–6

I remember the first time it happened to one of my friends. Her husband had
committed adultery. His betrayal crushed her, and rightly so. Her life was turned
upside down by his sin. Unfaithfulness truly has awful consequences.

Tragically, since that day, I've seen this happen over and over again in the lives
of people around me—and in my own life as well. No, I have not committed
adultery, and neither has my husband. But we've both been unfaithful more times
than we like to admit—unfaithful to the God who has given us so much and who
deserves our full allegiance. And so, most likely, have you.

That hurts to admit, doesn't it? It's hard to think of ourselves as unfaithful. But
who of us can say we are without sin and have obeyed God perfectly—even
though we are the bride of Christ? We are not faithful to God—at least not every
minute of every day.

Our unfaithfulness looks like bowing to our idols, putting other things in our life
ahead of God. It looks like neglecting to commune with Him through prayer. It
looks like stubborn unrepentance, refusing to acknowledge our sin and come to
Him for forgiveness and reconciliation. If we're honest with ourselves, we can see
we just don't have it in us. We lack the faithfulness required to keep a relationship
with God.

But thankfully—although we should not neglect pursuing a relationship with
God—our faithfulness isn't what keeps us with Him. It's *His* faithfulness that se-
cures us. And it is Jesus' righteousness that causes our Lord to see our faithlessness
as faithfulness.

God is faithful. And God's faithfulness means that even though we fail, even though we selfishly pursue our own desires instead of His, He will never forsake us. God's faithfulness means that His love endures forever. He *will* finish the good work He began in us. He is faithful because He has said so.

This passage in Romans 3 is interesting in that Paul is speaking of Jews who have not obeyed God. He is reminding them that God has a covenant relationship with them and God will be faithful to keep that covenant. God's faithfulness to keep His promises is also not dependent on our faithfulness to Him. Though we waver, doubt, and wander, He never has and never will.

For the Christian it is deeply encouraging to remember God's faithfulness as we battle condemnation, fear, regret, and shame. We will mess up. That's just a given. We will be unfaithful to our faithful God.

But God does not let our faithfulness (or lack of it) determine our standing before Him. Instead, God looks to His perfect Son. We could never manage what Jesus has done for us—perfect faithfulness, perfect obedience, perfect trust—but He has accomplished it for us. And one day, Jesus will return to present us, His bride, as pure to a holy God.

REFLECT

1.   List some specific ways you have been unfaithful to God in recent weeks or months. (Try to be honest.) Did you find this exercise difficult? Why or why not?

2.   How has Jesus been faithful in those areas where you've been unfaithful? For example, this week I spoke sharply in anger to one of my children. In so doing, I was unfaithful because I sinned against my child and ultimately against God. (Our sin is always ultimately against God.) Jesus, however, is

pure, and His love is pure. Even when He could crush us with His power and might, He doesn't (Isa. 42:2–3). Thankfully, it is this Jesus who is interceding for me. I confessed my sin and received His grace.

3. Why is it so important to reflect on the faithfulness of God?

4. Write down some specific ways that you've seen God be faithful in your life.

5. For further study, read Romans 9–11, where Paul unpacks how God is faithful to the Jews while also maintaining that not all will believe. In what ways does that passage enrich this one?

WEEK ONE | DAY THREE

READ | ROMANS 5

RESPOND

1. The first word of this chapter in the ESV and other translations is *therefore,* which indicates that the first line in chapter 5 follows on what Paul was helping us see in chapter 4. Summarize chapter 4, and then put this first line in your own words.

2. Why is it that we can "rejoice in hope" (5:2)?

3. What does it mean that Christ died for us "while we were still weak" (5:6 ESV)? (Hint: Paul is not speaking about our physical ability.)

4. We've learned about God as righteous and as the Justifier. In this chapter we see another attribute of God displayed. What attribute do you see described in 5:6–11?

5. At the beginning of verse 12, we see Paul use the word *therefore* again. What is being summed up here?

6. In verses 12–17, the phrase "the free gift" (or "gift" in other translations) is repeated several times in contrast to what happened with Adam, "the first man." What is this free gift, and why is it being contrasted to the work of Adam?

7. The final *therefore* in chapter 5 (found in verse 18) significantly sums up the power of the gospel. (Other translations use "So then" or "consequently," but the idea is the same.) What, according to Paul, has Jesus accomplished?

8. What does it mean for grace to abound (or increase) in 5:20?

EXPLORE

For Sinners

For while we were still weak, at the right time Christ died for the ungodly. For one will scarcely die for a righteous person—though perhaps for a good person one would dare even to die—but God shows his love for us in that while we were still sinners, Christ died for us.
ROMANS 5:6-8

"Helicopter mom" is a term that refers to a mother who hovers over her children, often in a worried way, and never allows them to explore on their own. I would not consider myself a helicopter mom; I'm more like the shield that Captain America holds. I encourage my kids to explore and play, but I position myself to protect them from danger. If we are walking down the sidewalk, I make sure I'm between them and the road. If we cross the street, I step out into the road first and stop as if to say, "Car, you would have to plow me down before you get to my kids."

The truth is, I would do anything to protect my kids from harm. I wholeheartedly believe that I would die for them if necessary. And I guess that makes sense. After all, I gave birth to them and experienced the rush of hormones that bonded us together. I've invested countless hours of my life in their care and feeding. I've snuggled with them and played with them and taught them. They are part of our family's legacy and the fabric of our daily life. I love them, and they love me back. They even obey me from time to time. (If I were on social media, I would add a big smile emoji here.)

My desire to protect my kids makes sense. But why would Jesus do what He did for us?

The Scriptures describe Jesus as a man who was "despised and rejected" by people, a "man of sorrows" who was "despised" and not "esteemed" (Isa. 53:3). He was not considered a hero by the world's definition and standards. He was nothing—and treated as nothing—to the world He chose to enter and the majority of people He encountered.

And yet Jesus died for them. Jesus went to the cross for people who are and were opposed to Him. He died for people who were not seeking Him and people who accepted Him but then went on to live their lives as if He didn't matter. For all of these—and for you and me—Jesus chose to suffer and die:

> He has borne our griefs
>   and carried our sorrows. . . .
> he was pierced for our transgressions;
>   he was crushed for our iniquities.
> (Isa. 53:4–6)

This is the ultimate display of God's love for us. While we were still content in our sin, Jesus died to rescue us from it.

There are a number of reasons why I would die for my kids. There is absolutely no reason why Jesus should have died for you and me except for His great love and mercy. There is nothing that we contribute to the initial relationship with our Savior except our sin.

How can this possibly be good news? Because it tells us that we don't have to clean ourselves up in order to be acceptable to Jesus. He accepts us on His own terms— terms that included death and resurrection. And then He invites each of us to come to Him and submit our lives to Him. He didn't come for the righteous, He came for sinners. That's you and me. This is God's great love to us.

REFLECT

1. What are some characteristics of a person you might consider risking your life for?

2. Have you ever considered all of Jesus' suffering beyond His death on the cross (man of sorrows, rejected, etc.)? Take some time to meditate on that suffering. How does doing so affect you?

3. How is God's love on display in Romans 5:6–8?

4. How might the knowledge that Jesus died for His enemies and for those who were not seeking Him affect the way you live now?

WEEK ONE | DAY FOUR

READ | ROMANS 6

RESPOND

1. Paul is emphatic with his rhetorical question found in 6:1 (and repeated in 6:15). Why should we take sin seriously? Why should we take grace seriously?

2. What does the symbolism of baptism represent in 6:2–4?

3. According to Paul, what are some of the ways that knowledge of the resurrection affects how we live?

4. What is the significance of the word *death,* which is found in 6:1–4? Why are the words *death, dying,* and *died* repeated in this passage?

5.   How is it that you were once a slave to sin?

6.   What is sanctification (6:19)? Paul uses the word *leading* to reference sanctification. Why would it be good to remember that this verse suggests a pursuit or a path and *not* an arrival?

EXPLORE

Sin No More

What shall we say then? Are we to continue in sin that grace may abound? By no means! How can we who died to sin still live in it? Do you not know that all of us who have been baptized into Christ Jesus were baptized into his death? We were buried therefore with him by baptism into death, in order that, just as Christ was raised from the dead by the glory of the Father, we too might walk in newness of life.
ROMANS 6:1–4

It's a popular, oft-quoted Bible story, told in John 8:1–11. Scribes and Pharisees bring to Jesus a woman who has been caught in the very act of adultery. They want to stone her and are evidently testing Jesus to see if He, too, will join in their condemnation. Confronted with their testing, Jesus throws it back to them: "Let him who is without sin among you be the first to throw a stone at her." Of course, no one can throw a stone because they are aware of the law, and they know they have sin in their lives. To execute judgment on the woman would be to declare their own perfection. As a result, no one condemns the woman, and neither does Jesus. Instead, He says to her, "Go, and from now on sin no more."

There is some debate as to whether this story was a part of John's writing and the original manuscript.[4] Nevertheless, there is much we can glean from this passage that relates to Romans 6.

The Jews were afraid that Paul's teaching on grace would lead people to continue in their sin. If it is true that we are saved by grace and by faith and that salvation is not based on our good works, then what's the point of saying no to sin? Paul emphatically argues that it is precisely the grace and mercy of Christ that leads us to say no to sin.

As we see in the John 8 story, Jesus does not forgive the woman and then say, "Go live as you wish" or "Keep on living as you have been." He does forgive her sin. He does not condemn her or hold her sin against her. He pours out abundant grace. And He then tells her to "go, and from now on sin no more."

Similarly, once we taste the goodness and grace of God, we are motivated to say no to sin and empowered by the Spirit to do it. Yes, our sin is forgiven. Yes, it is not held against us. But we have died with Christ and been raised to life. We are a new creation—we are in Christ. This leads to newness of life, not greater death in sin. Like the woman caught in adultery, when we turn from our old self and are born again, we are motivated and empowered to go and sin no more.

Ah, but there's a catch, right? We still sin!

The reality is, even in our newness of life, we still battle temptation every day, and sometimes we give in to it. But there's a difference between sometimes losing a skirmish and just giving up the battle—excusing our sin because of the grace of God.

Because we are Christ's, we keep on fighting sin, knowing that grace is available when we fail. Grace truly is amazing; it covers every sinful thought and deed. But at the same time, we never want to take advantage of God's grace.

---

4. Some of the original Greek manuscripts do not include John 7:53–8:11. If you look in both the NIV and ESV translations, you'll see that these verses are bracketed off, with an explanation that some manuscripts do not include these texts. For more information on the inerrancy and sufficiency of Scripture, I suggest reading Kevin DeYoung, *Taking God at His Word: Why the Bible is Knowable, Necessary, and Enough, and What That Means for You and Me* (Wheaton, IL: Crossway, 2014). For a helpful historical analysis of the New Testament, I recommend *Canon Revisited: Establishing the Origins and Authority of the New Testament Books* (Wheaton, IL: Crossway, 2012).

When we take God's amazing grace seriously, when we understand what it cost, we have to take sin seriously too. By God's grace, and only by His grace, you and I can fight temptation. And *because* of that grace, compelled by God's love, we'll keep trying our hardest to "go and sin no more."

That's my charge to you today. Keep fighting, not because you earn God's favor, but because you already have it.

REFLECT

1. How would you define grace? How have you experienced it in your life?

2. What are some of the struggles you have faced as you have walked in newness of life? What kinds of temptations tend to pull at you? Have these changed over the years?

3. What are some practical strategies that might help you take both grace and sin seriously as you walk out your faith? What has helped you in the past to move closer to "sinning no more"?

WEEK ONE | DAY FIVE

READ | ROMANS 7

RESPOND

1. According to this passage, what does it mean to belong to Jesus (7:1–6)?

2. What is the "law" that Paul refers to in Romans 7? What law?

3. Why does Paul emphasize that the law is not sin (7:7)? What, according to Paul, is the purpose of the law?

4. In this chapter we again see the seriousness of sin. It also seems that Paul is careful about how we judge the law (7:13). Why might that be?

5. What battle does Paul describe in 7:13–23?

6.   What does Paul mean when he writes that he serves the law of God with his mind, but serves the law of sin with his flesh (7:25)? What does he mean by "flesh"? (Hint: it is not just our physical bodies or the part of us that craves something like food or sexual intimacy.)

EXPLORE

I **Want** *to Do Right!*

So I find it to be a law that when I want to do right, evil lies close at hand. For I delight in the law of God, in my inner being, but I see in my members another law waging war against the law of my mind and making me captive to the law of sin that dwells in my members. Wretched man that I am! Who will deliver me from this body of death? Thanks be to God through Jesus Christ our Lord! So then, I myself serve the law of God with my mind, but with my flesh I serve the law of sin.
ROMANS 7:21–25

We've all been there. We've all tried *really* hard to do the right thing and then . . . failed.

Consider these different scenarios:

- You and your spouse begin a discussion, and you say to yourself, *I am going to listen. I will not get angry.* Then, the next thing you know, you are in a full-on, heated conflict because you yelled in anger.

- You are serving in your church because you genuinely love the people who make up the congregation, but you also secretly hope for recognition.

- You have tried hard to practice self-control, but just a slight glance at that man takes you down a road of fantasy and lustful imagination.

- You are hanging with a group of friends who are gossiping, and you know in your heart that it's wrong, but you just can't resist knowing that secret too.

What's going on in each of these instances? Paul lays it out for us in Romans 7—when we want to do good, sin is close by.

I know this all too well in my own life. For those of us who have the Spirit inside of us, there is a real internal struggle, a battle that we go through on a daily (and often even hourly) basis. Paul rightly describes this battle as a war between the truth we know in our hearts and minds and the desires of our flesh. These two aspects of our being are waging war against one another.

Acknowledging that there *is* a war is an initial safeguard against our sin. When we rightly understand that we struggle with what is sometimes called indwelling sin—the presence (and temptation) of sin in our lives that continues even after we are saved—then we can fight it with the power of the Spirit.

The danger in concentrating on our sin, however, is that we can be drawn into becoming too introspective, focusing so much on our sin that this focus paralyzes us from doing good. Don't let the fear of sin overpower you; do and pursue good anyway.

We will have this internal battle to fight for the rest of our lives, but we have a God who has given us His Spirit as a weapon. And just as Paul reminds us at the end of this section of Scripture, we too must remind ourselves that Jesus covers our sin.

Who will deliver us from our struggle with sin? Jesus, that's who. And He not only delivers us, but also stands in our place. Although we will battle sin for the remainder of our earthly lives, the cosmic battle has been won. Jesus has defeated sin and death. We are seen as righteous and don't stand condemned by our sin.

Remember all those scenarios describing the waging war within us? In Christ, it is as if you and I have pure motives, good intentions, perfect self-control. This is a miracle that we ourselves have experienced—and Jesus has accomplished it for us through His death and resurrection. Yes, thanks be to God through Jesus Christ our Lord!

REFLECT

1. Do you remember a time when you experienced this war between the flesh and the redeemed heart and mind that knows what's true, right, and good? What were the circumstances? How was the struggle resolved? In what ways do you still struggle?

2. Have you ever been hesitant to do or say something good because you were afraid of doing or saying it for the wrong reasons? Did you manage to overcome that fear? How?

3. Why is it important to guard against too much introspection about sin? What could happen? Do you think we should also guard against not being introspective enough? Why or why not?

4. If you have time, read back through the first seven chapters of Romans. What concepts stand out most for you in these chapters? Which have the most relevance to you in your daily life? Keep these thoughts in mind as we move on into Romans 8, which is the real focus of this book.

SHIFTING GEARS

The format of this study now changes slightly as we concentrate on a smaller number of verses per week. From now on you are going to get your introduction and "Respond" questions at the beginning of each week's lesson since we are looking at a smaller number of verses each day. You will still have a short devotional and "Reflect" questions each day.

life in the spirit

When sitcoms or cartoons portray someone trying to choose between good and evil, they often show a little "devil" sitting on one of that person's shoulders and a little "angel" sitting on the other. It's kind of silly and certainly not real, but it does represent how you and I feel at times. It's as if there's one voice in our ear telling us the right way to go and another trying to lead us astray, and we feel the tension of trying to hear the right voice and walk the right way. It's not easy!

If we are Christ followers, of course, we want to "walk by the Spirit" (see Galatians 5:16 and 25). But we can only do that when we are enabled and empowered by the Holy Spirit Himself!

But this isn't just a matter of choosing between our inner "devils" and "angels." It's a matter of learning to live in the strength and wisdom of our Savior. And for that we are given a supernatural Helper—the Holy Spirit.

Isn't that incredible news? God doesn't call us to do something without providing the grace for us to do it. He calls us to this walk, but He also enables it. And if we want to listen to the Lord and hear the Spirit, we must ask God for help.

In this week's text, we will be looking at what it means to have life in the Spirit.

READ | **ROMANS 8:1–11**

RESPOND

(These are the core Bible study questions you'll work through this week.)

1. In Romans 8:1, we see that word *therefore* again. What is this *therefore* referring to? Why is it important as we read the rest of the passage?

2. Paul uses the word *law* several times in verses 2–8. Go through and find these. Note that not all instances of this word refer to the same law! What different kinds of laws does Paul mention in this chapter?

3. The word *flesh* is mentioned several times as well. List the various descriptions or attributes of "the flesh."

4. Paul emphasizes the mind in this passage. Why do you think he does that? What does this emphasis tell us about our walk and how the mind affects it?

5.   What do you think this text might have meant to the people who received this letter?

6.   Where is Jesus in these verses? Where do you see the gospel?

7.   What do you learn about God and His character in these verses?

8.   How might you apply these verses to your life?

WEEK TWO | DAY ONE

EXPLORE

No Condemnation

There is therefore now no condemnation for those who are in Christ Jesus.
ROMANS 8:1

We come to Romans 8 knowing there's a battle going on inside us. Like Paul we have that ragged old sin clinging to us to the point that we often do wrong even when we want to do right (Rom. 7:21–24). With Paul, we plead in utter frustration, "Who will deliver me from this body of death?" (Rom 7:24). And, wonderfully, we have the answer: "Jesus Christ our Lord!" (7:25).

God has made a way for us through Jesus, and we know this is true. And yet so often we still stand condemned in our own minds and in our own hearts.

To be condemned is a fearful thing. It means to be declared unworthy or even evil, to be judged and declared guilty. Condemnation is an expression of the strongest disapproval. It's not something any of us would want from anyone—especially God.

But God tells us in His Word that there is *no* condemnation for those in Christ Jesus. That means that if you are found in Christ, God does not disapprove of you. In fact, His response to you is just the opposite. God not only approves of you, He even counts you as righteous because of His Son.

To be sure, your sin deserves condemnation. All the sin you and I have committed and will ever commit deserves condemnation. But God poured it all onto Jesus so that those who believe in Him would never experience condemnation. And because of that, we don't have to condemn ourselves. We don't have to continue to ask God to forgive us for this sin or that sin that keeps nagging at our conscience if we have already asked for His forgiveness. We don't have to hide from Him for fear that He will find out the parts of us that are unworthy or shameful. Today, even though it may be hard to believe, we can rejoice in knowing that God rejoices over us because of Jesus.

Isn't it good news that God doesn't hold our sins against us, that He doesn't deal with us according to our transgressions (Ps. 32:2; 103:10)? That He doesn't bring up our past or remind us of our faults? That we face no condemnation because of what Jesus has done for us?

And keep in mind that *no* means no. No condemnation doesn't mean there's *almost* no condemnation or just a little of it. *No* means none, zero, not an ounce of condemnation to be found because of the blood of the Lamb. As far as the east is from the west is how far He removes our sin from us—an evidence of His steadfast and enduring love (Ps. 103:11–12).

An implication of receiving this amazing grace is that we in turn can experience the freedom of forgiveness from others and the freedom to extend that same forgiveness. Another is that our obedience takes on a completely different character. Tim Keller explains that "Christians who don't understand 'no condemnation' only obey out of fear and duty."[5] We must preach this to ourselves every single day. Because we are not condemned, our obedience can grow out of our love for the Savior and reverence for the Father. Today ask the Lord to give you the freedom to stand in His grace.

5. Keller, *Romans 8–16 for You*, 13.

REFLECT

1. Why is the word *therefore* important to the first line of Romans 8? (Most translations include it.) What implication does this word have concerning the declaration that there is "no condemnation for those who are in Christ"?

2. Why do you think Paul uses the word *now* in 8:1 instead of simply saying, "There is therefore no condemnation"? Why is the inclusion of this word important?

3. Saying that "there is no condemnation for those who are in Christ" implies that there *is* condemnation for those who are *not* in Christ. What form does that condemnation take? Why are those who are in Christ not condemned?

4. What does it mean to be "in Christ"?

5. Do you ever struggle to rest in or fully accept the truth that you are not condemned? Why or why not? If you do struggle, what specifically do you tend to struggle with?

6. Spend a moment praying the truth found in this Scripture. Ask the Lord to give you faith to believe there truly is no condemnation for those who are in Christ Jesus.

WEEK TWO | DAY TWO

EXPLORE

Freedom in the Spirit

For the law of the Spirit of life has set you free in Christ Jesus from the law of sin and death. For God has done what the law, weakened by the flesh, could not do. By sending his own Son in the likeness of sinful flesh and for sin, he condemned sin in the flesh, in order that the righteous requirement of the law might be fulfilled in us, who walk not according to the flesh but according to the Spirit.

ROMANS 8:2-4

I was a very active and involved student in high school and college, participating in anything from band (flute) to track and field (sprinter) and just about everything in between. But while I excelled at many of these pursuits, I was never the best at the physically challenging ones. Most often I came in second. And the interesting thing about my consistent second place was that it wasn't due to lack of effort or desire. I *wanted* to be first. I never missed a track practice (although I will admit that my heart wasn't always in it—running is hard!). I did everything I could to make myself better, but it didn't seem to make any difference.

These days, of course, I can look back with a healthier perspective and appreciate both my accomplishments and the skills I acquired. But back then, the fact that I just couldn't seem to make that coveted top spot was a huge frustration to me.

I wonder if we sometimes approach the Christian life the way I approached my activities back in school. We try to be perfect. We pursue and strive and run until we are weary, but we never can seem to make ourselves perfectly clean, totally pure, always loving, perfectly obedient. Our striving never leads us to perfection . . . so we end up feeling like failures. We may even be tempted to give up trying to live the way Jesus taught us to. If we can't ever get it right, what's the point?

This is similar to the "law of sin" that Paul talks about in Romans 8:2. Here he is not referring to the so-called Mosaic law—the commandments given to the Hebrew people through Moses in Exodus, Deuteronomy, Leviticus, and the like. (He will talk about that law in verse 4.) Instead, he is addressing the power of sin over our lives. Sin has such power over our flesh that it acts like a law: try as we might, we can't stop ourselves from following it.

Even the Mosaic law can't break the power of this "law of sin." The Mosaic law *reveals* sin to our hearts and minds, but it can't stop us from sinning. So instead of freeing us, the Mosaic law actually condemns us. Knowing a problem without being able to change it is the very definition of helplessness!

Just as my striving for perfection in my activities never got me to first place, we can never obey the law perfectly. Try it for a day, an hour, even a minute, and you'll quickly see you can't do this Christian life by your own righteousness. And there is no one without sin: "If we say we have no sin, we deceive ourselves, and the truth is not in us" (1 John 1:8). We can never obey the law perfectly.

So you and I have a problem. No matter how hard we try, we will come up short because of the power of sin in our lives. On our own—in our flesh—we have no hope of pleasing a holy and perfect God.

Thank God for Jesus. God sent His Son to do what the law could never do and what our flesh could never do. Jesus fulfilled the law's righteous requirement, which is perfection. Jesus is the only perfect One. He is the only One who could make a way for us to the Father—by making the ultimate sacrifice on our behalf.

A fresh knowledge of our need for salvation through Jesus can transform how we walk through this life of ours. Walking by the flesh—trying to get through on our own strength—leads to weariness, discouragement, and ultimately sin. We don't trust Jesus for our salvation and then do the rest in our own strength. We trust Jesus for the rest of our lives—for every step of our Christian walk. Walk in Him, walk by the Spirit, and put away any striving in your own flesh.

REFLECT

1. What does it mean that the (Mosaic) law was weakened by flesh? How is that possible?

2. Why is it a good thing to have our sin revealed to us?

3. Have you ever tried to obey God perfectly? What happened? Do you ever sense yourself striving for "Christian perfection"? If so, why? If not, why not?

4. What are some telltale signs that you are walking in the flesh and attempting to attain righteousness on your own? What are signs that you are walking in the Spirit? How does reflecting on Jesus' sacrifice on your behalf help you pursue righteousness and walk in the Spirit?

WEEK TWO | DAY THREE

EXPLORE

Setting Our Minds on the Spirit

For those who live according to the flesh set their minds on the things of the flesh, but those who live according to the Spirit set their minds on the things of the Spirit. For to set the mind on the flesh is death, but to set the mind on the Spirit is life and peace. For the mind that is set on the flesh is hostile to God, for it does not submit to God's law; indeed, it cannot. Those who are in the flesh cannot please God.
ROMANS 8:5–8

Recently I lay down in bed, happy for the chance to relax and rest up for a new day. I stretched out and got comfortable, only to find my mind was running in circles. I began to worry about a conversation I needed to have. I mentally ran down a list of items I needed to accomplish the next day. I remembered an item I needed to purchase, and I thought about the few things I had forgotten to accomplish that day.

I quickly realized I wasn't relaxed at all. My body was attempting to rest, but my mind just would not slow down. And to make things worse, my runaway thoughts were full of anxiety. Would that conversation I needed to have go well? Would I be able to accomplish all I needed to the next day? Would those things I forgot to do today bring me trouble? My anxious thoughts almost pushed me out of bed to work, even though I knew I needed rest (Ps. 127:2).

It's no accident that Jesus commands us to love God with our heart, soul, *and* mind. I can safely say that most of my sin originates in my mind, from what I think, and a lot of it stays there. I imagine that's true of most of us. We know how to act, and there are a number of things we likely wouldn't do just for fear of what others might think. But our minds are another story. No one sees what we are thinking—at least, that's the lie we tell ourselves. We can have vengeful, angry thoughts; we can lust; we can be anxious; we can judge others—all within the confines of our mind. We don't have to say a word or move a finger to sin.

God knows every hair on our heads—and what's inside our heads, too. He knows that we need not only transformed action, but also transformed thoughts. Paul warns us that the mind set on the flesh leads to death. As we've already learned, this is because the flesh is rotten with sin. So the mind set on the flesh is the mind set on sin. The mind set on the flesh isn't thinking about the things of God. It's not thinking about God at all!

I'll share another story to illustrate this point further. During a particularly hard season of my life, I found myself in a conflict with a girlfriend and wasn't sure how I would be able to work it out. I was nervous about our future conversations, so I began to visualize how one might go. I wanted to make sure I would listen to her well. But as I started imagining how that might go, I also imagined what she might say—and I found myself growing angry. Within seconds, I was imagining how I might stick it to her with a sharp reply. My mind was making up a scenario that hadn't happened and—by the grace of God—wouldn't happen. But just imagining that scene led to a physical response. My heart sped up. My breathing became heavier. I was ready for a fight. *Yikes!*

That's the kind of thing that happens when we set our minds on the things of the flesh, letting our natural human tendencies rule the way we think. The result is anxiety, fear, and conflict—especially if we let our thoughts dictate our actions—and eventually death, because that is the natural end of living in the flesh.

In contrast, setting the mind on the Spirit leads to life and peace. As Isaiah wrote (26:3),

> You keep him in perfect peace
> > whose mind is stayed on you,
> > because he trusts in you.

The Spirit also enables us to love, as Paul describes so memorably in 1 Corinthians 13:4–7:

> Love is patient and kind; love does not envy or boast; it is not arrogant or rude. It does not insist on its own way; it is not irritable or resentful; it does not rejoice at wrongdoing, but rejoices with the truth. Love bears all things, believes all things, hopes all things, endures all things.

Had my mind been set on the Spirit during that difficult time, I would surely have responded differently. I would have withheld judgment; after all, I didn't know what she would actually say. I would have been able to resist imagining a comeback. And I would have ultimately loved my sister in my mind and heart and been able to live in peace.

Let's train our minds, as Paul (inspired by the Holy Spirit) instructs us, to think on things that are true, honorable, just, pure, lovely, commendable, excellent, and worthy of praise (Phil. 4:8). The mind set on the Spirit is set on good and holy things. And the mind set on the Spirit knows when to take those worrisome thoughts to the Lord and submit them there.

Ask God to give you self-control in your mind and to fix your eyes and mind on the good and perfect One.

REFLECT

1. Think for a moment if you've ever been particularly anxious about something. Where did that anxiety originate?

2. Do you believe that what we think is as important as what we do? Why or why not?

3. What does setting your mind on the Spirit actually mean?

4. What kinds of circumstances in your life tend to pull your thinking in fleshly directions? What are some practical ways you might fight that tendency and actively set your mind on the Spirit?

WEEK TWO | DAY FOUR

EXPLORE

The Spirit in You

You, however, are not in the flesh but in the Spirit, if in fact the Spirit of God dwells in you. Anyone who does not have the Spirit of Christ does not belong to him. But if Christ is in you, although the body is dead because of sin, the Spirit is life because of righteousness.
ROMANS 8:9-10

I became a Christian at the age of twenty-two, which gave me a bit of time to do some sinning. Actually, I would have been considered a "good girl" even before that, although I struggled with various temptations. When I became a Christian, however, I was radically changed. My motives, ambitions, ideology, even desires were transformed. The Spirit was in me—changing my old self into a new creation (2 Cor. 5:17). This was nothing but miraculous!

Before becoming a Christian, I did not have the Spirit of Christ. (Christ was not in me, and I was not in Christ.) I did not belong to Him. Spiritually speaking, I was dead (Eph. 2:1)—dead in my sin. But God, who is rich in mercy, brought me to life. He gave me His Spirit and Christ's righteousness.

This is the experience of everyone who trusts in the finished work of Jesus Christ on their behalf. But something can happen after our conversion. It can happen after a few months or ten years down the road. We can be tempted to forget about the miracle work of grace and begin to notice all the things we do wrong. We can begin to confuse ourselves with our sin. We can even become more aware of sin than we do of God's grace.

It's good to be aware of our sin as long as that awareness leads us back to the cross. Knowing how deeply sinful we are should allow us to focus all the more on Jesus and produce in us a grateful heart. But it shouldn't allow us to forget that we are in Christ and that we have the Spirit dwelling in us, that we are a new creation. The flesh may be dead because of sin, but the Spirit is alive!

The Holy Spirit living in us testifies to a new and transformed life. Miraculously, God looks on us and sees the righteousness of Christ (Col. 3:3, 2 Cor. 5:21). And that can be hard to understand. How can a God who knows everything in our hearts—even the bad stuff—still see us as righteous?

The answer is grace—merciful, amazing, stunning, incomprehensible grace. God freely chooses to see Christ's righteousness in us when we choose to come to Him. And then we have the pleasure of fighting sin by the Spirit, secure in the grace that comes with our salvation.

Christ in us creates the potential for joy-filled, abundant life.

REFLECT

1. Why does Paul use the word *however* in verse 9? What significance does it have for understanding your life in the Spirit? (Note: to answer these questions, you may need to go back and read the verses before this one.)

2. Do you remember the moment when you came to Christ? If so, describe the transformation that took place. If you don't remember exactly when it happened (for some people, it was a gradual process), think of a time when you experienced significant spiritual growth or change and describe that experience.

3. The devotional describes several things that can happen to us after our conversion. Have you experienced any of these in your own life? Which ones? Have you noticed any other significant changes in the years since your conversion?

4. If you are a Christian, you are no longer dead in your trespasses and sins. How can you strike a balance between being aware of your sins—and fighting them—while remembering that you are alive with Christ?

EXPLORE

Life to Mortal Bodies

If the Spirit of him who raised Jesus from the dead dwells in you, he who raised Christ Jesus from the dead will also give life to your mortal bodies through his Spirit who dwells in you.
ROMANS 8:11

I've always been interested in athletics and physical training and participated in sports most of my life. I didn't play traditional sports like basketball, but until college I was very involved with gymnastics and track and field. Then, knowing that collegiate sports wouldn't be in my future, I became a group fitness instructor. I was a fitness professional for many years. I taught things like Pilates, weight lifting, and high intensity conditioning. Not surprisingly, for many years I was in pretty good physical shape.

As the years have gone by, however, I've slowed down. I still work out, but my aches and pains tend to extend for longer than a few hours after a workout. Recently I've developed a painful heel condition called plantar fasciitis that hurts terribly and makes it difficult to even walk at times.

I imagine that anyone who is getting older can easily relate to this experience. But as someone who has always been active, I'm acutely aware of the physical effects of aging, which remind me of my own mortality. In other words, I can feel the effects of the fall, which brought in death,[6] almost daily.

The gospel, however, is good news not only for our souls, but also for our bodies. God's work in our lives affects every aspect of us, as we see in verse 11. Paul tells us something remarkable here: the power that raised Jesus from the dead is the same that lives in us. Which means that when we are in Christ, we too will be raised from the dead by the power of the Spirit!

If you are thinking, *How could this be true?* I join you in that wonder. Every time I think about the gospel and all its implications, I find myself asking, as David did in Psalm 8:5,

> What is man that you are mindful of him,
>   and the son of man that you care for him?

I think that's exactly what Paul was getting at in Romans 8:11. He used the mind-blowing reality of the resurrection to emphasize just how powerful and trustworthy God is. It's as if Paul was saying, "Seriously, guys, if God would do *this*"—raise Jesus from the dead—"then surely you can trust Him to do *this* too"—resurrect our mortal bodies.

Have you ever heard the acronym YOLO? It's not as popular as it once was, but for a time it seemed everyone was using it. YOLO stands for "You Only Live Once." And so often we live our lives as if this were true. But if we take Romans 8:11 to heart, everything changes.

If I believed that YOLO was my reality, perhaps I would despair as I experience the deterioration of my physical body. If I only live once, then there's no good purpose in the aches and pains. If I only live once, then how I respond to trials and struggles and other pain doesn't matter. I might even wonder, *I only live once, so why bother trying to care for my body? I'm dying anyway!*

6. The fall, sometimes referred to as the fall of man, refers to when sin entered the world, as described in Genesis 2 and 3. Adam's failure brought both spiritual death and physical death to humankind.

But if I believe Paul, that we live on beyond our death and will have resurrected and fully restored bodies, life here in the body does matter. As Tim Keller helps us understand,

> The Christian has a body that is decaying (v. 10), yet also enjoys a spirit, a mind, that is alive. And, Paul says, not only must our spirits/minds not follow our flesh now, but one day our flesh will follow our spirit. In Greek thought, the physical was bad, to be rejected and hopefully one day to be left behind; the spiritual was good, to be embraced. Verse 11 overturns all this. . . . Someday, even our bodies will be totally renewed and made eternally alive by the Spirit.[7]

Knowing we will live forever should motivate us to live with eternity in mind. Just as we are working to care for our souls, we must work to care for our bodies. This means, in part, that we will think about what we do to and in the body. We will consider that our bodies are temples of the Holy Spirit, that the Spirit dwells in us (1 Cor. 3:16–17; 6:19–20).

With eternity in mind, we remember that bodily training, though not ultimately important, does have some value. For example, it allows us to serve others (1 Tim. 4:8). With eternity in mind, we accept our responsibility to be living sacrifices, not being conformed to this world but renewing our minds (Rom. 12:1–2). And with eternity in mind, we remember that whatever we do in the body—whether it's eating or drinking or working out or whatever—we seek to do to the glory of God (1 Cor. 10:31).

Even in our bodies we are not living for ourselves. We consider the Spirit that dwells in us and the sacrifice of Jesus on our behalf. And we remember with joy that one day our mortal bodies, which are gifts from God, will be fully renewed and restored.

---

7. Keller, *Romans 8–16 for You*, 11.

REFLECT

1. The Spirit testifies to us that we are new. How does remembering this new life both now (spiritually) and in the new life to come (both spiritually and physically) affect how you live today?

2. What are practical ways we might care for our minds and bodies today as we wait for the new life to come?

3. Read 1 Corinthians 15:35–38 and Philippians 3:20–21. How do these passages add to what Romans 8:11 has to say about our resurrected bodies?

heirs with Christ—God's children

Living according to the flesh leads to death, but life in the Spirit leads to just that—life. Part of our motivation for pursuing a life led by the Spirit is understanding that we are not our own. And included in this understanding is the choice to submit to our great God. We have been bought with a price. We are God's children—no longer slaves, but heirs with Christ. And one day we will join in His reign.

READ | **ROMANS 8:12–17**

RESPOND

(These are the core Bible study questions you'll work through this week.)

1.   In these short verses, how many times is the Spirit referenced? What is the significance of the Spirit's work here?

2. Who lives according to the flesh? Who lives according to the Spirit? And what is the effect of both life in the Spirit and life in the flesh?

3. Paul in verse 13 tells us to "put to death the deeds of the body." (A theological word for this process is *mortification*). What are the deeds of the body (see Col. 3:5)? Why do you think Paul uses the word *body* here instead of *flesh*? Is he saying that our physical bodies are inherently bad?

4. What does the presence of the Spirit in our lives indicate about us (see Rom. 8:16; 8:19; 9:8; 9:26; John 1:12)?

5. If you did not receive a spirit of slavery, what did you receive? What does it mean to "receive" the Spirit?

6. Verse 15 refers to "a spirit of slavery" and falling "back into fear." Slavery to what (Gal. 2:4; Heb. 2:15; 1 John 4:18)? And fear of what exactly?

7.   Research the word *Abba*. What is its origin? Where is it used in the Bible other than in Romans?

8.   To be an heir is a place of privilege and typically involves receiving a spiritual or physical legacy. What, according to Paul, is the inheritance we will receive as children of God?

9.   According to verse 17, what condition must we meet in order to be God's heirs and Christ's co-heirs? Why might Paul remind us of this right after sharing about our privileged place with God the Father?

10. Where is Jesus in these verses? Where do you see the gospel?

11. What do you learn about God and His character in these verses?

12. How might you apply these verses to your life?

WEEK THREE | DAY ONE

EXPLORE

Debtors to Mercy

*So then, brethren, we are under obligation, not to the flesh, to live according
to the flesh—for if you are living according to the flesh, you must die, but if
by the Spirit you are putting to death the deeds of the body, you will live.*
ROMANS 8:12–13 NASB

Have you ever committed to do something that you realized later carried extra
obligations? I have. My husband and I promised our son that if he earned enough
money, he could purchase a reptile. We figured it might or might not happen, but
either way it would take him a while to earn the money.

It took him one month! So before we knew it, we were bringing home a bearded
dragon lizard—and learning the additional obligations this purchase entailed:

- We had to clean out the lizard's cage.

- We had to feed it live crickets and keep those crickets alive long enough to
  be eaten.

- We had to pay for the lizard's care, which cost far more than just the purchase price.

In this case, even the additional obligations turned out to be a joy. Seeing our son beam with gladness and watching him learn how to care for one of God's creatures has been a true pleasure. But maybe you have felt a different kind of obligation that has sent you down a path that wasn't good or pleasant.

Sin has a way of making us feel obligated to it, for instance. We start down a path and think we must submit to it. *What's the use*, you may think, *I'm going to fail anyway. Why bother trying to fight the desire. It's too great.* Or even more sinister: *I deserve this thing that is wrong, so I'm going to do it.*

But we see here in Romans 8:12 that we are under obligation ("debtors" in the ESV) not to sin, but to the Spirit. We do not have to submit to our flesh because we have the Spirit and are ruled by the Spirit; we have no obligation to the flesh. And that means we can say no to sin.

Paul puts this another way in 1 Corinthians 10:13: "No temptation has overtaken you that is not common to man. God is faithful, and he will not let you be tempted beyond your ability, but with the temptation he will also provide the way of escape, that you may be able to endure it."

This Scripture assures us of two things: 1) we will be tempted to sin, and 2) we will always have a way out, a way to say no. We are guaranteed this because of Jesus' death and resurrection. So next time you feel like you must give in to the sin that clings so close to you, the sin that is telling you that you have no choice but to give in, remember that you are in Christ, you have the Holy Spirit, and you are not obligated to sin. Your obligation is now to the Spirit, not the flesh, so you and I can live free of the bondage of sin.

REFLECT

1. What does it mean to "live according to the flesh"? In what ways might you "die" if you live this way?

2. How does living according to the Spirit bring life?

3. Think of a time when you a) gave in to sin because you felt there was no way out, or b) were tempted to sin but experienced the way of escape. What happened? What did you learn from this experience?

WEEK THREE | DAY TWO

EXPLORE

Children of God, Led by the Spirit

For all who are led by the Spirit of God are sons of God.
ROMANS 8:14

"On your mark, get set, go!" With that, my father and I raced across a parking lot, as we had done so many times in the past. This time was different, however. This time, for the first time, Daddy's little girl had become faster. My little feet turned over more quickly, hitting the pavement at lightning speed. Okay, perhaps I'm exaggerating a little, but it felt like lightning speed to me. With a jolt of excitement and enthusiasm I cheered, "I won!" And my defeated dad cheered too. He was proud of his girl.

That's the story of so much of my young life. My dad was my best friend. He was my greatest support and cheerleader and my most trusted confidant. And then, in 1997, my father passed from this life to the next. I was nineteen years old. The phone call letting me know he was gone was one of the worst calls I've ever received.

My father had a way of making you feel like you were the most important person in the world. I was his little girl. I belonged to him. It wouldn't be until the age of twenty-two that I would feel that sense of belonging again. That was when I became a Christian. I now belonged to God—God, the Father. And so do you if you've put your trust in Christ for your salvation.

The doctrine of adoption—that Christians are added to the family of God and become His beloved children—is one of the most comforting aspects of Christian theology and the reality of our faith. My earthly father was very present, available, and encouraging, but even he pales in comparison to the awesome, ever-present, always faithful, pure and good God. And if your relationship with your earthly father was less than ideal, God is so much better. Perhaps you had an absentee father or even an abusive one. If you have placed your faith and hope in the finished work of Jesus, you now have an infinitely loving, infinitely wise, infinitely dependable Father.

I submitted to and obeyed my earthly father. I respected his authority in my life. Of course I didn't do this perfectly (hardly!). But when my dad would say something, I usually listened. That was one sign that he was my father!

In a greater way, as we are led by the Spirit to submit to God, our submission is evidence that we are His. That check you get in your spirit when you've done something wrong or that jubilation you experience when you sing songs of praise to the Lord are both clues about who you belong to. You are not your own. You've been bought with a price, and you are being reassured of that through the Spirit within you.

Likewise, God treats us as His very own. Hebrews reminds us that we are not illegitimate children, but rather full children of God (Heb. 12:8). This means that He not only gives us good things, but also disciplines us through revelation of sin and restores us just as a loving earthly father would. Our response to this discipline and restoration is again by the Spirit. The Spirit enables us to accept and respond to our Father's work in our hearts.

Today, if you sense that nudge in your spirit or that influx of joy—rejoice in knowing that you are not an illegitimate child, but a true child of God. Ask God to make clear the good and righteous steps to take, being led by the Spirit as you walk in a manner worthy of the gospel.

REFLECT

1. What is your own experience of an earthly father? How has it helped or hindered your feelings toward your heavenly Father?

2. Have you ever felt or do you often feel the "nudges" this author speaks of? Describe a time in your life when you felt this. What are some ways we can become more responsive to the Spirit?

3. How does being led by the Spirit and being a child of God correlate?

WEEK THREE | DAY THREE

EXPLORE

No Longer Slaves

For you did not receive the spirit of slavery to fall back into fear, but you have received the Spirit of adoption as sons, by whom we cry, "Abba! Father!"
ROMANS 8:15

Anytime, anytime while I was a slave, if one minute's freedom had been offered to me, and I had been told I must die at the end of that minute, I would have taken it—just to stand one minute on God's earth a free woman—I would.
ELIZABETH FREEMAN

My mind struggles to understand slavery. I can't imagine what it must have been like to wake up chained—metaphorically or literally—and owned by another human being. When my mind goes there, when I allow myself to try to put my feet in a slave's shoes, I all but fall down in sorrow.

Slavery was an atrocious institution in the early days of our country, and it didn't exist only in the South. A slave named Elizabeth Freeman actually took the new state of Massachusetts to court, seeking to be freed. She fought for her freedom. And she won! She became the first African-American slave to be set free under Massachusetts law and is credited with informally abolishing slavery in the state.

Elizabeth Freeman's burning desire to stand on the earth for even one minute as a free woman isn't hard to imagine. And once she tasted the sweetness of freedom, surely she would never, ever have desired to return to slavery.

And yet we sometimes do just that, in a sense. Though we are free in Christ, time and time again our hearts return to that time when we were slaves to our flesh, slaves to our fears, slaves to the law and the law's demands on us. We fall back into old, fearful ways of thinking. In this text we see Paul reminding the church that God doesn't want that for us. God desires our freedom—and He provides it through His Son and through our adoption as His children (8:15).

To the first-century church, this reminder of freedom from slavery would have great significance. Slavery was a daily reality in that culture, so people in that day would instantly understand the analogy of being released from slavery and not falling back into it. Like Elizabeth Freeman, they knew in their bones that there was a big difference between being a slave in someone's household and being a free member of the family!

We may not witness slavery on a daily basis anymore, but Paul's analogy still holds powerful truth for us. We were once slaves to our sin (Rom. 6:20), but once we're in Christ this is no longer true. We do not have to submit or obey or entrust ourselves to those old ways. God has made us new, and as new creations we have the privilege of adoption. Now we are not only free, but children of almighty God. And not only children, but beloved children who can relate to our Father intimately.

It is no small thing that we can use the word *Abba* as we cry out to our Father. This Aramaic word for Father is an intimate term, even somewhat childlike—it could also be translated as "papa" or "daddy." Significantly, it is also the name Jesus used in addressing God.[8] It is a grace to us that we can cry out to the Lord in prayer in such intimate and personal ways. He gives us that access. Theologian Douglas Moo puts it this way: "In 'adopting' us, God has taken no half measures;

8. Leon Morris, *The Epistle to the Romans* (Grand Rapids, MI: Eerdmans, 1994), 315; Douglas J. Moo, *The Epistle to the Romans,* New International Commentary on the New Testament (Grand Rapids, MI: Eerdmans, 1996), 502.

we have been made full members of the family and partakers of all the privileges belonging to members of that family."[9]

Today remember this great access you have to your Abba. When you have to fight not to fall back into your old ways of thinking, cry out to your heavenly Father, who is available to you and listening. Remember that you are His, that you've been bought with a price. And that means you are truly free.

REFLECT

1. What kinds of "slavery" are you prone to fall back into? How can having the "spirit of adoption" help you avoid this?

2. What fear is Paul referring to in these verses?

3. How might understanding that we can call God our Abba impact how we approach Him? Do you feel comfortable approaching Him in such an intimate way? Why or why not?

4. Read Mark 14:36. What does it mean that we get to use the same name for God our Father that Jesus tenderly used in the garden of Gethsemane?

9. Moo, *Epistle to the Romans*, 503.

EXPLORE

The Spirit Provides Assurance

The Spirit himself bears witness with our spirit that we are children of God.
ROMANS 8:16

As I've mentioned before, my dad was one of my best friends. I never wondered if I was his child because I could see our family resemblance. I looked like him, and in so many ways I acted like him. But of course our bond was more than biological and more than environmental. I knew in the depth of my soul that I was Daddy's little girl. That I belonged to him.

Sadly, not everyone can say the same about their earthly fathers. Some men abandon their children, sons and daughters, leaving their families to fend for themselves. Other fathers stick around physically but remain emotionally absent. Some are addicts or abusive. Some become ill or even die and are unable to be there for their families. If any of this is true for you, you may have pushed against the idea of belonging to someone, especially a father, as a way to protect yourself from heartache.

But the message of Paul for all of us—for people like me whose earthly father was loving and dependable and for those whose fathers couldn't or wouldn't fulfill their obligations—is that in Christ we belong. We belong to God—our perfect Abba Father. And what's more, we *know* it.

This text tells us that the Spirit confirms to us that we are children of God. The Spirit bears witness with our spirit to prove that it is true. How does this work? Let me ask you a few questions:

- Have you ever been in a desperate situation and found yourself calling out to God as Father?

- Have you ever sensed that something you have done was wrong and then asked God for forgiveness?

- Have you ever rejoiced or felt comforted because you sensed God's nearness as a Father?

There are likely a number of questions I could ask. But if you've answered yes to any of these, then it's likely your spirit—prompted by His Spirit—is saying to you, "Daughter, you are His." You can do this because God "has put his seal on us and given us his Spirit in our hearts as a guarantee" (2 Cor. 1:22). Or as Derek Thomas puts it, "We cry. The Spirit cries. The Holy Spirit cries with our spirit (Rom. 8:16). This communion between us and the Spirit is the surest indication of our adoption as sons of God."[10]

All this is part of God's assurance to us. The bond between His Spirit and ours is a unique one, and we will see later in the chapter that it is absolutely secure. You won't want to cry out to God as Abba—an intimate, relational calling—if there isn't something in your spirit enabling that cry.

Today, with confidence and assurance, cry out to your Father. Even the greatest fathers on this earth (like mine!) do not compare with our Abba Father.

If you ever find yourself wondering where you belong, remember that if you have accepted Jesus, you belong to God the Father. You are His, and He is yours. There's nothing else you need.

10. Derek Thomas, *How the Gospel Brings Us All the Way Home* (Lake Mary, FL: Reformation Trust, 2011) loc. 583, Kindle.

REFLECT

1. In what ways has your experience with your earthly father (or father figure) shaped the way you think of God the Father?

2. What does it mean for the Spirit to bear witness?

3. In what ways have you experienced the Spirit bearing witness with your spirit?

4. We know that Jesus has made a way for us to boldly approach the throne of grace (Heb. 4:16). Yet have you ever struggled to have the confidence to approach Him? If so, why? Has this struggle changed in any way over the years?

WEEK THREE | DAY FIVE

EXPLORE

Suffering to Be Glorified

Provided we suffer with him in order that we may also be glorified with him.
ROMANS 8:17

In this verse, Paul is talking about how we walk out the Christian life, particularly as it involves suffering. Suffering with Jesus in modern-day America does not necessarily look like the suffering that would have occurred in the first-century church. Associating with Jesus then would have been downright dangerous. Walking out the faith, trusting in the finished work of Jesus would have put them in conflict with established Jewish or Greek or Roman customs. And proclaiming Christ publicly could have gotten them imprisoned, beaten, or even stoned (Acts 7:54–60).

Our call to suffer, in the American context, may be less risky in a physical sense, but in a society that is increasingly opposed to the things of God, our association with Christ and the things of Christ seems to be increasingly countercultural. We may well be required to take a stand on things that look increasingly foolish to the world. We may need to make decisions that are best for our souls but could force us to sacrifice comfort and ease. We may even experience deep rejection—from family, friends, neighbors, and coworkers—on account of our faith.

Whatever our suffering may be, we know that it doesn't entail abandonment from our Father. We don't suffer in vain. In fact, our suffering with Him results in our being glorified with Him. This is a part of what it means to follow Christ.

Paul reminded us of this earlier in the book of Romans: "Now if we have died with Christ, we believe that we will also live with him" (6:8). Our old self was crucified. Dead. It's gone. We are a new creation who lives with Christ. And part of this new life involves suffering: "For as we share abundantly in Christ's sufferings, so through Christ we share abundantly in comfort too" (2 Cor. 1:15).

Now, it would be extremely discouraging if our suffering were the end of the story. But suffering is *not* the end. Our suffering leads us somewhere and to Someone. To glory.

To be glorified with Christ means that we will be made perfect. We will be like Him—pure, sinless, and free of all pain and suffering. Even sickness will be gone. The sin that clings so close to each of us—gone. The pain of being set against the society around us—gone. Our present suffering—with Christ—leads us to our future hope, which we will look at fully in week four. Today we can face whatever may come our way, proclaiming Jesus and knowing that we have a future grace ahead of us—glory.

REFLECT

1. What are some of the ways you have suffered in the past or suffer now? In what ways does knowing that your suffering is temporary and has purpose change your outlook?

2. We are not able to suffer as Christ did, nor are we called to do so (crucified on a cross, bearing the wrath of God). So what does it mean to suffer *with* Christ? How might we do so?

3. What does it mean to be glorified with Christ? Is this only for the future, or do we partake in some of this today?

future glory

There will be suffering as we wait for the day when we are with Jesus forever. That's just a given. God's creation waits with groaning for all to be made right. We long to be away from this fallen world and these fallen, broken bodies. But we don't wait in vain. We have a Hope, and our Hope won't put us to shame. Our great Hope sympathizes with our weaknesses and sent a Helper to assist us in our need. We are weak, but He is strong. We cry out, and He will answer in our day of trouble.

READ | **ROMANS 8:18–27**

RESPOND

(These are the core Bible study questions you'll work through this week.)

1. This section of Scripture seems to take a bit of a leap from the previous one. Why do you think Paul reminds us of suffering right after sharing about our adoption and telling us that we are heirs with Christ . . . and before getting into the subject of glory?

2. Read 1 Corinthians 4:17 and compare it to what Paul says in Romans 8:18 about suffering. What do both of these verses say about the suffering we go through here on earth? How can that view transform our view of both suffering and the Christian life?

3. What might be the glory that will be revealed? (Hint: you may find the answer in the verses following this one.)

4. How is or how can creation be subject to futility? And who is Paul referring to when he writes, "because of *him* who subjected it" (v. 20, emphasis mine)?

5. How do the concepts of restoration, newness, rebirth, and renewal describe what creation will experience?

6. What does it mean to have the "firstfruits" of the Spirit (v. 23)?

7. Paul writes that we are eagerly waiting for adoption as sons (v. 23). How do you reconcile having already been adopted but still waiting for adoption?

8. How does waiting for the hope we haven't seen build patience (v. 25)?

9. What does "likewise" refer to in verse 26?

10. What does *intercede* mean? (Look it up.) In what ways does the Spirit do this for us (vv. 26–27)?

11. Where is Jesus in these verses? Where do you see the gospel?

12. What do you learn about God and His character in these verses?

13. How might you apply these verses to your life?

WEEK FOUR | DAY ONE

EXPLORE

Incomparable Glory

For I consider that the sufferings of this present time are not worth comparing with the glory that is to be revealed to us. For the creation waits with eager longing for the revealing of the sons of God.
ROMANS 8:18–19

I have a friend who got hit by a bus. Yes, you read that right. And she not only got hit by that bus, she survived to tell about it. I won't reveal her name or tell her story. That is her own story to tell. But one of the things that was remarkable to me was watching her work through the suffering and pain—literal, physical pain—that followed her accident.

My friend was others-focused during much of her recovery. She would ask friends to pray for others who were suffering in the rooms adjacent to hers. She would praise God and proclaim His goodness. And one time she even joked about being hit by a bus, pointing out how often we use the phrase, "I feel like I've been hit by a bus," and then it had actually happened to her!

Everyone suffers differently, and even as I reflect on my friend's whimsical response to her suffering, I want to make it clear that we are all free to experience our own pain differently. We don't have to be cheerful. As a matter of fact, many of the psalmists help us learn to lament with sorrow and weeping. As we'll see throughout this week of study, even nature is groaning as it waits for the Lord's returning.

And it wasn't that my friend had a façade of cheerfulness. There was something deeper going on in her spirit. She was suffering with joy. She had taken to heart the reality that no matter how we respond to our suffering, none of it compares to the joy we can look forward to if we are in Christ.

There have been times when my own suffering has felt so overwhelming and crushing that I struggled to remember that this world is not the end of the story, and my suffering won't have the last word. Suffering has a way of fogging up our vision for the future. But something in us knows that there's something better, somewhere better. The whole creation—us included—longs for the future day when we will experience freedom from all our suffering.

So, if the Word tells us that our suffering doesn't compare to the glory that will be revealed, why don't you and I take a moment to compare?

Suffering	Glory
We suffer because of our sin.	We will be sinless.
We suffer because of the sins of others.	Evil will be banished, so there will be no more sin.
We suffer from worry and anxiety.	There will be nothing to worry about, and our risen bodies and minds will not be subject to anxiety.
We suffer because of sickness.	There will be no more sickness.
We suffer from living in a fallen world where we are subject to natural disasters.	There will be a new heaven and a new earth.
We suffer because of sorrows.	There will be no more tears.
We suffer because of death.	Death will be vanquished.

Don't you want to get there? That longing for something else, for something better, is built into you because you were made for glory—for heaven. And knowing *that* can inform the way we suffer today. Paul tells us clearly that our present suffering doesn't compare to the glory we will one day experience. Knowing this future glory allows us to suffer well—in other words, we suffer with hope.

Today, by God's grace and through His Spirit, remember that your future isn't just bright—it's glorious! Glory awaits you at the end of your suffering. That longing you sense is glory calling you by name. It's a good thing as long as it is coupled with hope. May God give you grace and faith to face your present suffering because tomorrow it will be finished.

REFLECT

1. How do you tend to respond to suffering in your life? Does the *kind* of suffering make a difference (physical, emotional; deserved, undeserved)?

2. Do you ever experience a longing for something better? When do you think that longing can cross over into sinful discontentment?

3. How might knowing our future affect how we suffer?

4. The biblical concept of glory might be hard for us to comprehend if we only look at the English dictionary. For example, the English word *glory* might mean to take pride or pleasure in something. But the Greek word translated *glory* in the context of Romans 8 means the bliss of heaven. In other places in Scripture it means the fullness of God. How does the biblical definition of *glory* help us read Romans 8:18–19 differently? Rewrite these two verses, substituting the definition of the word *glory*.

5. List areas in your life that bring you suffering now but that will be healed by this future grace. Be as specific as you can—not just "broken relationships" (for example), but "my relationship with Mom;" not just "sickness," but "my arthritis;" not just "injustice," but "being passed over at work." Rejoice in knowing that these things will one day be healed or restored. If you wish, read through your list several times during the week.

WEEK FOUR | DAY TWO

EXPLORE

Suffering and God's Creation

For the creation was subjected to futility, not willingly, but because of him who subjected it, in hope that the creation itself will be set free from its bondage to corruption and obtain the freedom of the glory of the children of God. For we know that the whole creation has been groaning together in the pains of childbirth until now.
ROMANS 8:20–22

I can definitely relate to what Paul describes here regarding the pains of childbirth. I've never felt anything quite like giving birth. I don't want to frighten my friends here reading, but yes, childbirth is a special kind of painful. To put it plainly, God wasn't playing around when he said that women would have pain in bringing forth children (Gen. 3:16).

According to Paul, this is exactly the type of pain that all of creation is experiencing as it waits to be freed of the fall. Nothing is right on this earth. Everything is broken and affected by the fall. Even the mountains are crying out for freedom from corruption.

This doesn't mean we don't experience joy here. Oh, we do! Even with childbirth, the pain and struggle involved in growing a human in the womb and then bringing him or her into the world doesn't compare to the moment you hold that little human. Even for those who adopt, there's a longing and waiting and often painful experience until the moment they hold their child.

Jesus used this same analogy of childbirth to instruct His disciples and help them understand both the waiting they'd endure after His death and the reward that would follow:

> When a woman is giving birth, she has sorrow because her hour has come, but when she has delivered the baby, she no longer remembers the anguish, for joy that a human being has been born into the world. So also you have sorrow now, but I will see you again, and your hearts will rejoice, and no one will take your joy from you. (John 16:21–22)

Jesus was saying that our earthly sorrows are temporary. Our groaning and pain have an expiration date. One day it will all be over. But meanwhile the pain and the groaning are real. Jesus never said otherwise. But He also said that we'll forget all about our pain when we finally see Him face to face. I don't know about you, but that brings me great hope and joy!

And yes, I know we aren't there yet. Right now, in fact, you are likely experiencing the kind of groaning that the earth endures too. One day, just like creation, we will be free of this painful waiting. We'll also be free from those aspects of life on earth that seem "subjected to futility"—that is, pointless or useless or meaningless.

One day we will be liberated completely from the bondage of this world. Free—totally and completely. So let's wait with hope.

REFLECT

1. The pain of childbirth is a vivid and powerful example of pain that produces something meaningful or wonderful, but it's not the only possible one. Can you think of other painful or difficult experiences that produce similar results?

2. What are some signs we can see right now that creation is groaning, waiting to be free of corruption?

3. What aspects of life on earth could seem futile or meaningless from a human perspective? (Hint: see Ecclesiastes 1.) How do God's promises to us change that?

WEEK FOUR | DAY THREE

EXPLORE

Hope for What We Do Not See

And not only the creation, but we ourselves, who have the firstfruits of the Spirit, groan inwardly as we wait eagerly for adoption as sons, the redemption of our bodies. For in this hope we were saved. Now hope that is seen is not hope. For who hopes for what he sees? But if we hope for what we do not see, we wait for it with patience.
ROMANS 8:23–25

- "I hope to see you soon."

- "I hope he remembers to pick up the lemons from the grocery store."

- "I hope I get that job."

- "I hope my boss doesn't find out what I did."

- "I hope he asks me to marry him."

How often do you use the word *hope* in a single day? Probably a lot. And even if you don't *say* it, how often do you think it?

Most of us spend a little time hoping for something. We do it even without realizing what we are doing. And this hope we experience daily can be negative or positive. That is, we can hope that something good will happen or that something bad won't happen. In the Scriptures, however, we rarely find hope used in a negative way. The hope we find in Scripture—including the hope we find in Romans 8:23–25—is one of anticipation and the expectation of something good. And it's a hope we can count on, unlike a lot of our earthly hopes and dreams.

As I write this paragraph, in fact, the song lyrics flowing through my earbuds are upbeat and hopeful: "We have found something worth living for." The song, of course—and the hope—is about a romantic relationship. The singers are anticipating a future full of exciting and invigorating love for one another. But while this love they sing about is sweet, the truth is, it will eventually let them down. Even if they defy the odds and manage to stay together, they both will eventually die and leave each other.

Romantic love on earth, as wonderful as it can be, is simply not worthy of our full hope. Expectation and desire for good? Absolutely. But to put our *hope* in another sinner's ability to love us perfectly will surely leave us discouraged. Placing our hope in anything on this earth—love, wealth, knowledge—will always leave us longing. As it should.

You and I might fall into a silent trap of placing our hope in earthly things because, like other people, they seem tangible. We can see them, touch them, experience them, hold onto or even hoard them. We don't have to wait for an indefinite future. When things feel awful, we can try to fill the void with food or purchases or whatever else we run to when we feel the groaning and pain of this world. But it doesn't work. It just leaves us continually longing.

So what is worth our full hope?

Jesus is our only hope, and it is through Jesus that we have the promise of eternal life. Our hope is not something we can see or touch or experience or hold—

except perhaps in brief glimpses and the promises of Scripture. No one can give an account of what it is like to be glorified in heaven with our Savior. We must wait patiently on this revelation. And yet we wait as people who know the end of the story is going to be good. We wait with a trustworthy hope. And we know that our everlasting, true, and pure Hope will never let us down or put us to shame (Rom. 5:5).

REFLECT

1.   What are earthly things or people you are tempted (or have been tempted) to put your hope in? Why will these things ultimately let you down?

2.   Does the fact that everything on earth will ultimately let us down mean that we should never trust anyone or invest in relationships? How can we live our lives deeply and fully while putting our ultimate hope in Jesus?

3.   What are some reasons we might find it difficult to wait for and hope in the Lord?

4.   In what ways have you seen the Lord be faithful even in the waiting?

5. What does "we know the end of the story" mean? What *is* the end of the story?

6. What aspects of Jesus' character secure our understanding that He will never let us down and we can hope in Him?

WEEK FOUR | DAY FOUR

EXPLORE

Our Help in Weakness

Likewise the Spirit helps us in our weakness. For we do not know what to pray for as we ought, but the Spirit himself intercedes for us with groanings too deep for words.
ROMANS 8:26

During my early years as a Christian, I was mentored by a sweet couple whose family, in the days when we were often together, grew from four people to eight! My dear friends—I'll call them Anthony and April—brought six kids into the world, and watching them manage and care for their family had a huge impact on the way I now care for my own children. And their influence on me goes way beyond that. My love for hospitality, my desire to get into the Word and grow in understanding it, even the way I view other people—all these have been shaped by this wonderful man and woman.

Anthony and April lived a simple life—not perfect, of course, but filled with peace and sweet joy. But then suffering hit them in the roughest and foulest way. Anthony was diagnosed with cancer and, after a few years of treatment and what looked like potential remission, he lost his battle, leaving April and their six kids behind. They knew he was with the Lord, fully healed and in no more pain. But here on earth he was absent, and his family felt that absence acutely.

When I went to his funeral I experienced something that has only happened to me a handful of times: I found myself completely and utterly without words. You think that in moments like that you'll be able to come up with *something*. But I was too sad, and I knew April didn't need Christian platitudes (even if I could think of some!). So I looked at April, clearly grief-stricken but yet glimmering with hope, and said, "I don't know what to say." She looked back at me and said, "I know."

Sometimes, maybe even often, our pain or confusion is so deep, we can't even come up with the words to express it, either to others or to God Himself. And God has a word for us in these times of mute groaning. According to His holy Word, we don't have to have the right words to say. When we are unable to find the words or even the coherent thoughts to pray to our Father, we can come to Him as we are, and the Holy Spirit will intercede on our behalf.

We don't need to try to be stronger than we are to come to the Lord. He invites us to come to Him in our weakness. And we don't have to come up with lofty words—or any words at all. Weary, weak, deeply affected by the wounds of this world—those are our qualifications for coming to God. He invites you and me to draw close, and then we can simply let the Spirit tell the Lord what He already knows we feel and what we truly need.

Don't hesitate to call on His name, even if all you can say is "Jesus."

REFLECT

1.   Have you ever had a difficult experience that left you speechless? Or have you ever tried to comfort a friend but didn't have the words to say? What did you do? Would you do or say anything differently now?

2.   Do you ever feel as if you must have certain words to come to God? Why or why not?

3.   Some Christians who find their words failing when approaching God use the words of others—the psalms, a book of prayers, or the like—to help them pray. Some find it helps to write out their prayers in a journal instead of simply speaking them. How do you feel about these approaches to prayer? What has helped you?

WEEK FOUR | DAY FIVE

EXPLORE

Interceding According to His Will

And he who searches hearts knows what is the mind of the Spirit, because the Spirit intercedes for the saints according to the will of God.
ROMANS 8:27

I've prayed a lot of prayers throughout the years. Some have been answered and others seemingly have not. I'm aware, however, that "unanswered" prayers are often prayers that have been answered in ways I wasn't expecting or hoping for. Because I know that God works for good in all things, I trust Him for those unexpected answers. And then there are the prayers that I reflect on later and thank God fervently that my wisdom is not His wisdom and my thoughts are not His thoughts (Isa. 55:8–9). Thank you, God, for those unanswered prayers!

Romans 8:27 is an interesting text. When I read it, a part of me thinks I ought to never try to pray using my own words again. That isn't the intent of the Scripture, of course. But there is something in it that causes me to pause and reflect on the Spirit's ability to intercede perfectly on our behalf. What power; what grace!

When we just don't know what to say or ask, the Spirit intercedes on our behalf with the exact request that the Lord will answer in the affirmative because it is "according to the will of God."[11] When our groaning is too deep for words, we can

---

11. Wayne Grudem, gen. ed., *ESV Study Bible* (Wheaton, IL: Crossway, 2008), 2171 (note on Romans 8:27).

trust that God knows and hears and understands exactly what we need. When we are confused and don't know what to ask, we can trust that He knows our need and is listening to the Spirit. As Derek Thomas writes, "Prayers that are badly expressed; prayers that are not really expressed at all; prayers that are just longings, aspirations, or groans—these prayers are 'fixed' on their way up to our Father."[12] This gives us such freedom to approach God at any time, in any way.

I don't know about you, but that makes me want to run to my heavenly Father. Maybe we can go to Him and simply say, "Lord, I don't know what to say or what is best or how to fix this, but I know You know, and so I ask You now to help me however You choose, according to Your will."

Right now if you are without words to say to the Lord but still long to speak to Him, know that the Spirit is interceding perfectly for you. Even the prayers you don't know how to pray are reaching Him, and He will respond in love.

REFLECT

1.   Have you ever seen your unanswered prayers work out for your good? What happened?

2.   Have you ever experienced answers to prayers you never actually prayed (a circumstance changed, growth in an area, or so on)? What happened?

12. Derek W. H. Thomas, *How the Gospel Brings Us All the Way Home* (Orlando, FL: Reformation Trust, 2011), 87.

3. Why do you think the Spirit is able to intercede with the exact prayer needed and according to God's will?

our assurance

We wait for our future hope with the promise that all things work together for good. God is good, and we rest in the assurance that He knew us before the foundation of the world. How encouraging to know that the God who knew and called us is also transforming us from one degree of glory to the next and that it's all a free gift of His grace. He called us from out of the pit—He saved us. Jesus paid it all, and you and I are justified (declared righteous) because of this payment. In the astonishing mystery and precious gift of God's grace, He views us just as if we've always obeyed Him.

READD | ROMANS 8:28–30

RESPOND

(These are the core Bible study questions you'll work through this week.)

1. This week is unique in that I'd like you to do a little word study. Look up each of the following words in a Bible dictionary, a concordance, an online study tool, or other study aid. (Remember, your Bible may have these tools built in.) Then answer the questions listed below each word. (We've already looked at or even defined a couple of these words, but doing them again can help deepen your understanding.)

WORD #1: *CALLED*

- Where does this word appear in the New Testament (besides Romans 8)?

- What is the origin of this word (if applicable)?

- What does this word mean in a New Testament context? (Write out a definition in your own words.)

- How does this word connect with the others on the list (and below)?

- What does this word tell us about salvation and the gospel?

- What does this word tell us about Jesus?

WORD #2: *FOREKNEW*

- Where does this word appear in the New Testament (besides Romans 8)?

- What is the origin of this word (if applicable)?

- What does this word mean in a New Testament context? (Write out a definition in your own words.)

- How does this word connect with the others in the list?

- What does this word tell us about salvation and the gospel?

- What does this word tell us about Jesus?

WORD #3: *PREDESTINED*

- Where does this word appear in the New Testament (besides Romans 8)?

- What is the origin of this word (if applicable)?

- What does this word mean in a New Testament context? (Write out a definition in your own words.)

- How does this word connect with the others in the list?

- What does this word tell us about salvation and the gospel?

- What does this word tell us about Jesus?

WORD #4: *CONFORMED*

- Where does this word appear in the New Testament (besides Romans 8)?

- What is the origin of this word (if applicable)?

- What does this word mean in a New Testament context? (Write out a definition in your own words.)

- How does this word connect with the others in the list?

- What does this word tell us about salvation and the gospel?

- What does this word tell us about Jesus?

WORD #5: *JUSTIFIED*

- Where does this word appear in the New Testament (besides Romans 8)?

- What is the origin of this word (if applicable)?

- What does this word mean in a New Testament context? (Write out a definition in your own words.)

- How does this word connect with the others in the list?

- What does this word tell us about salvation and the gospel?

- What does this word tell us about Jesus?

WORD #6: *GLORIFIED*

- Where does this word appear in the New Testament (besides Romans 8)?

- What is the origin of this word (if applicable)?

- What does this word mean in a New Testament context? (Write out a definition in your own words.)

- How does this word connect with the others in the list?

- What does this word tell us about salvation and the gospel?

- What does this word tell us about Jesus?

2. What is Paul referring to as "good" in Romans 8:28–30? In other words, what are the good things God is working together for us?

3. Where is Jesus in these verses? Where do you see the gospel?

4. What do you learn about God and His character in these verses?

5. How might you apply these verses to your life?

WEEK FIVE | DAY ONE

EXPLORE

All Things for Our Good

And we know that for those who love God all things work together for good,
for those who are called according to his purpose.
ROMANS 8:28

Often when we think of the word *good,* our minds typically go straight to our happiness and well-being. God's goodness to us must mean, we imagine, that He will make our lives easier or more pleasant and that everything will turn out the way we want it. But some years back I experienced a time when I knew that God was working all things for my good, but it looked and felt much more like death.

I had been praying that the Lord would help me with a relational conflict. I knew that I needed help, but I had no idea how to solve this particular problem. I was lost and confused. Why was this so hard? None of my other relationships had been quite like this one, so trying to work it out was more complicated than I'd ever imagined.

Then God answered my prayers—by seeing things rip apart. Bit by bit, it all came undone. Tensions grew and grew, and I was pretty sure that things would be irreconcilable on this earth.

But wait—is that even Christian? Can relationships really be unreconciled and glorify God?

The final outcome is, of course, in God's hands, and I do know that God moves in mysterious ways, and I have seen the unmistakable signs of His work during this time. The Lord has taught me things about myself I wouldn't have known were in the depths of my heart. Fear needed to be brought to the surface. I needed to be trained in the art of forgiveness and learn to bear all things in love. God really was working all things together for my good, conforming me to the image of His Son. And yet the outcome wasn't what I hoped for.

The "good" that Paul speaks of in Romans 8:28 has long been debated by scholars and theologians because the apostle does not fully spell out what he means. What we do know is that the text surrounding this verse points to the Spirit's intercession, God's salvation, and our ultimate well-being in Christ. From this I think we can comfortably conclude that Paul is not referencing material rewards or pleasures that are apart from the Spirit's work in our lives. Ultimately what is good is first, the transformation that takes place in our hearts as we walk out our faith, and second, the glory that is to come.

Today you may be living through a situation that simply doesn't seem good, and yet your heavenly Father is whispering, "Oh, dear one, trust Me!" He knows all things and is indeed working all things for the good of those who love Him. He is not withholding good from you. It isn't in His character to do so. Even what might appear like death will one day be revealed as His ultimate good in your life.

REFLECT

1. Have you ever experienced something that seemed awful at the time but that turned out to be good? What was it?

2. Have you ever had a time when you doubted God's goodness? How did you fight to trust and believe Him?

3. How might you define "all things" and "good"?

4. What are specific ways you see God working in your life right now? What are areas of your life where you need to trust Him because you can't see what He's doing?

WEEK FIVE | DAY TWO

EXPLORE

Our Assurance of This Good

For those whom he foreknew he also predestined to be conformed to the image of his Son.
ROMANS 8:29

My husband and I have a wonderful relationship, but like many couples we've had our fair share of disagreements. Most of these have, by the grace and mercy of God, only helped us understand each other better. We are both deeply aware of our desperate need for God. We know we are messed up and can't make it without Him. But through the years I have occasionally wondered if my husband would have chosen me had he known all he now knows about me. Would we have chosen one another? My gut feeling is yes, but I think that's likely biased. We love one another dearly, so it's hard to imagine not being together.

There's likely no one on this earth who knows me like my husband does. But God knows me better than anyone, even better than I know myself (Ps. 139:1–6, Rom. 8:27). God knows all of history—the beginning and the end (Ps. 90:4, Ps. 102:12, Isa. 40:10). He knows *my* history too—and yours.

This is good news for all of us, because it means God does not move in response to our moves. God has already moved. He already knows. His decision to rescue us isn't based on our good works or our faith or on anything we do, but on the work of a God who *foreknew* us before the foundation of the world (Eph. 1:4) and still is actively conforming us to the image of His Son.

Let us resist the temptation to judge or examine God as we would people. God will never leave us nor forsake us (Deut. 31:6) the way humans tend to do. In our earthly relationships, how we are valued or loved is usually in direct proportion to how we act or, even worse, to what we can do for or give to others. Not so with God. We are infinitely loved and valued no matter what. We are chosen because of His great love, and that love will be sustained to the very end.

Why will all things work together for our good? Because He foreknew us.

REFLECT

1. What human knows you better than anyone else?

2. The specific implications of God's foreknowledge have long been debated among theologians. Some would say, for instance, that He knows what will happen but that we ultimately make the decisions. Based on what you have seen so far, how would you reconcile God's foreknowledge of us with the concept of free will?[13]

3. How might being foreknown bring peace and joy? Is there anything about this idea that bothers you? If so, why?

13. For further study about free will, you can grab Scott Christensen's book *What about Free Will?: Reconciling Our Choices with God's Sovereignty* (Phillipsburg, NJ: P&R, 2016).

WEEK FIVE | DAY THREE

EXPLORE

Conformed to Christ's Image

For those whom he foreknew he also predestined to be conformed to the image of his Son.
ROMANS 8:29

Oh, man! I did it again. I got angry and said something I regretted. I lost control of my tongue, blurted out exactly what was on my mind, and ended up hurting someone.

Same situation but a few years later: Oh, man! I did it again. I got angry and almost said something I would regret, and although I didn't say it, I sure said a lot in my mind. I wanted to say it, but self-control enabled me not to say it out loud.

Same situation but a few years after that: Oh, man! I did it again. I got angry, but thankfully I was able to quickly pray and ask the Lord to give me peace and self-control. By the grace and mercy of God, I was able to take my thoughts captive and didn't lash out, either verbally or in my mind.

* * * * *

Have you ever thought to yourself or heard someone else ask, "When will I ever stop _____?" (insert habitual sin). When we become Christians we sometimes think that "freedom from sin" means we are completely free from sinning.

So when we become angry or lustful or envious, we might wonder if we are even Christians.

When we become Christians, we are miraculously transformed; we are new creations (2 Cor. 5:17). But we are not yet perfect. We have simply begun the process of becoming like Christ—conforming to His image. And because we are human, we will inevitably have bumps along that road. We will sin and have to wrestle with the consequences of our sin.

Paul wrote about this wrestling back in Romans 7:19, remember? "For I do not do the good I want, but the evil I do not want is what I keep on doing." And in Philippians 1:6 he assured us of God's promise to finish the good work He has begun in us. In other words, there's work yet to do in us, and there will be work to do until the day we are glorified and with Christ. Until then we will continue to be in the process of being conformed to Christ. Another word for this is *sanctified* (1 Peter 1:2).

Sanctification may feel like the scenarios I shared at the beginning of this devotional. It may be an excruciatingly slow-moving process, and we may only see progress in the long term, sometimes only in hindsight. You may never completely stop struggling with certain issues in your lifetime. But you can definitely become better at fighting sin.

Take anger, for example. You probably won't stop being angry, but you can become quicker to recognize that an angry response is about to well up inside you and quicker in responding so that the anger doesn't cause you to sin. (Remember that temptation is not the same as sin—see Hebrews 4:15). And even if it does, you can become quicker to respond to your sin appropriately by confessing it, seeking forgiveness, and trying to make amends.

Sanctification, in other words, is a lifelong process. But whether it happens quickly or slowly, whether we get there running or crawling, we are continually being changed and conformed to the image of Christ. God's Spirit is at work in your heart even now—yes, even though you failed in that problem area yet again.

At the most basic level, do you recognize that your failure was sin? If your answer is yes, right now you should thank and praise God for the work He is doing in your heart. You are no longer dead to your sin! And God will surely finish His work of sanctification in you. As Christ is holy, you (and I, too) will be made increasingly holy.

REFLECT

1. Is there an area in your life in which you'd like to see more growth? (I'll go first: I'd love to see continued growth in my struggle with fear.)

2. What are ways you've sought to deal with this area in your life?

3. How have you seen growth since you've recognized this problem area and started trying to grow in it? If you haven't seen growth, what might growth look like?

4. What aspects of Christ's image do you think we will be conformed to?

WEEK FIVE | DAY FOUR

EXPLORE

You Were Called to Salvation

And those whom he predestined he also called, and those whom he called he also justified, and those whom he justified he also glorified.
ROMANS 8:30

It's one of my favorite things to do—driving down an open, nearly deserted road, singing along with my favorite music or listening to an audiobook. Before I know it, I'm simply coasting, moving with the flow, while the landscape whizzes by me. It feels great—until those blue lights begin to spin in my rearview mirror and I realize I've coasted right into a speeding ticket. I've lost track of what was happening—lost my way, so to speak. And it took those sirens to wake me up, to jolt me out of my coasting coma. And although I don't see it this way at first (who wants a ticket?), being stopped if you are truly speeding can be a gift. That ticket might have prevented a much worse situation.

There are times in life when we need to be woken up out of our stupor. And there was never a greater time than the moment we were called into this great salvation. You and I were dead in our sins (Eph. 2:1). God sought us and called us into salvation.

But what does this have to do with coasting?

As I've gotten older, I've realized how easy it is to coast in the Christian life. It's so easy for us to get distracted with whatever it is we're doing and forget to remember Jesus. We might have a rhythm of going to church, even doing Bible studies like this one, but we may listen without ever truly worshiping. We may fall out of the habit of confessing sin or even praying because we just aren't thinking about it. We just coast along, doing Christian things but not really growing or becoming more like Jesus. And sometimes God puts sirens in our path to wake us up, but not always.

Sometimes we need to wake ourselves up.

If we desire to taste the goodness of God in all its fullness, we want to fight to remember that we were called. You and I can ask Him to *help* us remember! We can ask Him to keep us from growing too familiar with His amazing gift of salvation, to renew in us an excitement about His calling on our lives. We were dead in our sins, and now we have life; we were called by God, and now we are His. That's good news we must never allow ourselves to forget!

Today, if you are coasting, don't wait for the sirens to go off. Remember the good news of the gospel now.

REFLECT

1. Have you ever had a season of coasting in the Christian life—to use the cliché, going through the motions. What happened? Why?

2. What are some warning signs that we are coasting in our Christian lives? How can we recognize this in ourselves if God isn't sounding a "siren"?

3. How can remembering our calling and hearing the gospel again help us keep from coasting? What are some other ways we can "wake ourselves up" and renew our appreciation for what God has done for us?

WEEK FIVE | DAY FIVE

EXPLORE

Just as if You've Always Obeyed

And those whom he predestined he also called, and those whom he called he also justified, and those whom he justified he also glorified.
ROMANS 8:30

Justification is a legal declaration of our standing before the Lord. It is at this point that we trade in our unrighteousness for Jesus' righteousness (2 Cor. 5:21). We are only righteous (or just) before God through the work and person of Jesus Christ.

I've heard this explained in different ways. One is that once you and I have been justified, God views us as if we never sinned or as if we had always obeyed. That's pretty amazing, considering we not only *have* sinned and deserve the full punishment for it, but we *continue* to sin. This declaration of justification is an unspeakably generous, kind, and merciful gift of God's grace. It's also a picture of what we have to look forward to in the next life—glorification.

Right now, even though we have been redeemed, justified, and are in the process of being sanctified, there remains a great chasm between who we are now and who we will be when we are with Jesus. On this earth we may increasingly be able to obey God, follow Him, and rest in Him, but we will never once do any of it perfectly.

This shouldn't cause us to throw in the towel and give up. After all, we don't obey God because we will earn favor before Him; we obey out of love and reverence for Him. But it helps to remember that we have something even greater to look forward to. One day we will completely bear the image of Christ (1 Cor. 15:49). One day we will be glorified—completely free of sin, completely made holy.

I struggle to put words to this glorious truth. It's unimaginable. Did God really tell us, through His Word, that "we are God's children now, and what we will be has not yet appeared; but . . . when he appears we shall be like him, because we shall see him as he is" (1 John 3:2)? Yes! Yes, He did. The Bible is incredibly clear that one day we will not only be with Christ, we will be *like* Christ. We will be glorified. It's hard for me even to type that because I get overwhelmed by such good news.

Today, right now, we have work yet to do, but one day all the work for our growth in godliness will be done. It is finished, but it will one day be completed. This knowledge of our future glory should motivate us to love and serve the Savior every day. God is worthy of our admiration and worship because He is God, but the fact that He is good and gracious and has promised to glorify us motivates our pursuit of Him all the more.

REFLECT

1. What is the difference between justification and glorification? Why might it be important to not mix up the two concepts?

2. Why is it important to remember the work yet to be done in our hearts and minds?

3. Reflect on the statement above that "all the work for our growth . . . is finished but will one day be completed." What does that statement mean to you?

4. How does understanding our glorification help motivate us to live for Christ today?

everlasting love

What do we say to all these things we've learned over the past five weeks about God, His Son, His Spirit, and His everlasting love for us? It can all be summarized in Paul's unforgettable words: "If God is for us, who can be against us?"

If God could give His only Son for our sakes, then we can and should rest in the grace and assurance of our trustworthy Father's words to us. If we are in Christ, nothing at all can—or will—ever separate us from our Savior. What joy. What peace. What security.

This week we will finish off our study with some incredible news and assurance of our faith. Don't be daunted by the number of questions in the "Respond" section. That's simply because the last nine verses of Romans 8 are so rich and deep; there's a lot to unpack and consider. I think you'll find that even the questions are chock-full of the good news of the gospel. So let's dive in and see if we can't answer them all.

READ | **ROMANS 8:31–39**

RESPOND

(These are the core Bible study questions you'll work through this week.)

1. How many rhetorical questions does Paul ask in Romans 8:31–39? Is there any significance in the progression of Paul's questions? If so, what is it?

2. What are "these things" that Paul refers to in verse 31?

3. Using your concordance or Bible with cross references, what other verses in Scripture use language similar to that of verse 31 (God being for us)?

4. How does God giving over His Son secure our relationship with Him?

5. The phrase "all things" (v. 32) seems to encompass a lot. What are these "things"?

6.   What is the nature of the "charge" mentioned in verse 33? How does God's justifying us (v. 34) satisfy this charge? Why does Paul emphasize "God's elect" in this verse?

7.   Where else have we seen condemnation referenced in Romans 8? How is condemnation always remedied?

8.   Why do you think Paul emphasizes Jesus' defeat of death and also His position in heaven in verse 34? How does Jesus' position in heaven affect His ability to intercede for us?

9.   According to Romans 8 and other biblical texts, how has Christ displayed His love? Why is it good news that we can't be separated from this love?

10.   Why might Paul be highlighting suffering again in verses 36–37?

11.   What does it mean to be a conqueror (or more than a conqueror)? What does it *not* mean?

12. As we see in verse 37, victory does not come by our own strength and might. Rather, it is "through him who loved us." Where else in Scripture are we reminded of this reality (see, for example, Gal. 2:20, Eph. 5:2)?

13. "For I am sure" leaves no room for doubt or questioning as Paul concludes this chapter with assurance and confidence. Parse out the list of things we can be sure won't separate us from the love of Christ. Why can we be as certain as Paul was?

14. Where is Jesus in these verses? Where do you see the gospel?

15. What do you learn about God and His character in these verses?

16. How might you apply these verses to your life?

WEEK SIX | DAY ONE

EXPLORE

If God Is For Us . . . ?

What then shall we say to these things? If God is for us, who can be against us?
ROMANS 8:31

In my part of the United States (hello! The South), it's not unusual to see or be exposed to Bible verses every day. If you don't see one plastered on the back of a car, then you'll likely see it posted on social media. We see Scripture on mugs, T-shirts, and pretty designed squares posted on Pinterest. But I sometimes wonder if those of us who post them or repeat those verses actually *know* them.

I'm not talking about their context or even their interpretation, per se. I'm asking, do we know God? Do we know His Son? And if we know Him, do we truly take Him at His Word?

The verse we are exploring today is one of the most quoted verses in the entire Bible. It's so familiar to those of us who have been Christians for a while. The question Paul poses to us here encompasses all we've learned about our great salvation from the beginning of this chapter, but it doesn't necessarily stop there. This is the culmination of the first half of the book of Romans; it could even be argued that when Paul writes of "these things," he's referring to everything from chapters 5–8 or even to the entire first half of the book. Thinking on the truths and blessings he's been exploring in his letter seems to elicit this joyous response in Paul and should elicit the same in all of us. We have such a great assurance through Jesus.

But, let's look at the verse just before Romans 8:31, as it alone gives us reason to rejoice. Consider "all these things": God predestined us, called us, justified us, and will glorify us. We are not second thoughts in the mind and heart of God. Before the foundation of the world, He had us in mind.

Here is just a taste of what we know about God:

- He is omnipotent (all powerful): "For nothing will be impossible with God" (Luke 1:37).

- He is immutable (unchanging): "For I the LORD do not change; therefore you, O children of Jacob, are not consumed" (Mal. 3:6).

- He is omniscient (all knowing): "Great is our LORD, and abundant in power; his understanding is beyond measure" (Ps. 147:5).

- He is holy (set apart and absolutely pure): "And one called to another and said: 'Holy, holy, holy is the LORD of hosts; the whole earth is full of his glory!'" (Isa. 6:3).

The message of Romans 8 is that God, who is awesome in every way, is on our side. Think about that. And not only is He on our side, He has also made a way for us to know Him intimately through salvation and His Son. If this is who God is (we've only scratched the surface here) and if we know just a little of what He has done (we'll spend eternity learning more)— if this is the God who is *for* us, who then really can be against us? No one. No opposition can ever succeed against us if God is on our side.

As Leon Morris says:

> [Paul's] entire correspondence is eloquent of the foes the Christian encounters constantly. He means that with God "for us" it makes not the slightest particle of difference who is against us. No foe can prevail against people who are supported by a God like that.[14]

That doesn't mean we won't encounter opposition, of course—from other people, from Satan, even from own hearts. Some of these "foes" may even cause us to doubt God and all He has said about us and Himself in His Word. But this opposition means nothing in comparison to what we have in Christ Jesus. With God fighting on our behalf, none of them has a chance.

REFLECT

1. What ideas from Romans 5 might relate to or correlate with this pronouncement that God is for us?

2. Why might meditating on the attributes of God give us reason for awe and provide us with a sense of security?

3. Have you ever felt like you were opposed by someone? Without gossiping (that is, naming the person or, worse, slandering or talking bad about him or her), reflect on how the opposition affected you. Were you able to rest

14. Leon Morris, *The Epistle to the Romans* (Grand Rapids, MI: Eerdmans, 2012, orig. pub. 1988), 335.

in the truth that God is for you? If so, how did it help you move past the situation? If not, how did the situation resolve itself? How do you think you might handle this situation differently today?

4.   How does God ultimately show that He is for us?

WEEK SIX | DAY TWO

EXPLORE

Will He Not Graciously Give Us All Things?

He who did not spare his own Son but gave him up for us all, how will he not also with him graciously give us all things?
ROMANS 8:32

Inquisitive and tender, vivacious and loyal—that is how I'd describe my son and daughter respectively. They are both intelligent and fun, undoubtedly two of the greatest gifts the Lord has given my husband and me. We couldn't love them more—which is why the stories of Abraham and Isaac and the ultimate sacrifice of Jesus are absolutely remarkable to me. I just can't imagine offering up my kids for anyone or for anything.

Imagine longing for the gift of a child, waiting patiently year after year, only to have your hopes disappointed. (For some of you, this isn't hard to imagine, because you are currently experiencing that ache in your heart.) That was Abraham and Sarah's experience for many decades, despite the fact that God had promised them offspring. But then, well into their old age, their son Isaac was born (Gen. 17:19–22; 21:1–7). They were both overjoyed—until God told Abraham to take Isaac and offer him as a burnt offering (Gen. 22:1–2).

What a scary thing to be asked to do! I'm pretty sure I couldn't have done it. But Abraham set out to obey God. He took Isaac up on a mountain, prepared to make the sacrifice, and was just about to kill Isaac when an angel of the Lord told him to stop (22:12). The angel directed Abraham to a ram as a substitute sacrifice (22:13), and Isaac's life was spared.

Can you imagine what life would have been like for Abraham and Sarah if Abraham had actually had to sacrifice Isaac? We know, because God tells us that they loved Isaac greatly, so we can imagine the loss would have been devastating. Abraham was a God-fearing man, but he was still a man and would surely have mourned for the rest of his life.

But Abraham did not have to give up his son Isaac. God spared him that. And yet God had an eternal plan to sacrifice His own Son for the sin of the world, and He didn't spare either Himself or Jesus.

It was a wrenching moment. Just before He died on the cross, Jesus cried out, "Eli, Eli, lema sabachthani?" which means, "My God, my God, why have you forsaken me?" (Matt. 27:46). His Father could no longer be in His presence because Jesus had taken our place and become "sin who knew no sin" (2 Cor. 5:21). This was the ultimate sacrifice.

To add salt to the Savior's wounds, Jesus didn't die for friends, for people who loved Him, or for the godly. Instead, He willingly died for wretched sinners:

> For while we were still weak, at the right time Christ died for the ungodly. For one will scarcely die for a righteous person—though perhaps for a good person one would dare even to die—but God shows his love for us in that while we were still sinners, Christ died for us. (Rom. 5:6–8)

In view of this great sacrifice, Paul asks an important rhetorical question in Romans 8:32: "He who did not spare his own Son, but gave him up for us all, how will he not also with him graciously give us all things?" There is no greater sacrifice than for a parent to give up a child—nothing. If God was willing to sacrifice His Son for us, why would we ever doubt anything else that God says or does? Why would we not trust His promise to give us "all things"?

Although I do believe that "all things" in our text refers to both physical and spiritual provision, I'd caution us not to assume that God is going to provide everything we want. Second Peter 1:3 clarifies this a little by telling us that God's power has "granted to us all things that pertain to life and godliness." In other words, God will provide all we *need,* and ultimately what we need most is a right relationship with God. That's exactly what God has provided through His Son. There is nothing we need that hasn't already been accomplished for us. Hallelujah!

You and I may sometimes have to fight to believe this. It's easy to say, but not to live out. We may sometimes need to pray, as yet another loving father once cried out to Jesus, "I believe; help my unbelief" (Mark 9:24). And the Lord understands this. He knows we sometimes struggle to believe Him, which is why He reminds us repeatedly through His Word to rest in the work that He has done. It's as if He is saying to us, "Come on! I have done what you could never do, and isn't that enough?"

It is enough. It's more than enough. May we be people who respond in gratitude and proclaim with confidence: "If God is for us"— and sent His only Son to die on a cross on our behalf—"who can be against us?"

REFLECT

1. In what ways does the story of Abraham and Isaac relate to God's sacrifice of Jesus, and in what ways does it not compare? How are these similarities and differences important to the story of redemption?

2.   Often when we think of the cross, we go straight to Jesus taking our sins away, but so much more was going on. Reflect on the full sacrifice the cross represents—including God's sacrifice of His Son, Jesus' pain in the garden of Gethsemane, and the last words of Jesus.

3.   What are some areas in which you struggle to believe the Lord? How does God help you with this struggle?

4.   How does God's sacrifice prove that He really is for us?

WEEK SIX | DAY THREE

EXPLORE

Who Shall Bring a Charge against God's Elect?

Who shall bring any charge against God's elect? It is God who justifies.
ROMANS 8:33

I remember the first—and hopefully the last—time I had to sit on a stand in a courtroom. I was testifying about a case, and what I said could determine the fate of the person on trial. Actually, he had already determined his fate when he did the wrong deed. He had already been convicted of the crime, and my testimony would help determine his punishment.

I never want to be in that position again. I would also hate to be on the receiving end of a criminal charge.

Here in our text, Paul uses this legal term to describe the experience of being confronted or accused before God. He is asking yet another rhetorical question: Who can bring a charge against God's elect? In other words, who can accuse those whom God has chosen? The answer is obviously "no one." But that doesn't mean that no one *attempts* to bring charges. In fact, we are charged one way or another almost daily.

Who brings these charges? I want to focus on two common sources of accusation that both Paul's readers and we ourselves have to fight against.

The first one who tries to charge us before God is Satan, who is actually called "the accuser" in the Bible (Zech. 3:1, Rev. 12:10). He goes around planting seeds of guilt and doubt. Right before Job was stripped of all he owned, Satan accused him of only following the Lord because of his wealth (Job 1:9–10). And Peter warns us of just how vicious Satan's accusations can be: "Be sober-minded; be watchful. Your adversary the devil prowls around like a roaring lion, seeking someone to devour" (1 Peter 5:8). This adversary wants us to stand charged and guilty to the very end. He wants us to stand before the Lord defeated.

And who is the second accuser? Our own hearts!

I am not talking about "godly grief" over sin that leads to repentance (2 Cor. 7:10). I'm talking about the false guilt and "worldly sorrow" that grows out of the assumption that we must perform for the approval of God, that failure is unacceptable, and that sin is unforgivable. If we fall for any of those lies, we may wrestle with self-accusation even before we set one foot onto the ground in the morning.

But none of those accusations carry any weight before God—not if we are in Christ! Whoever accuses us—even ourselves—and whatever charges are brought against us, we can rest in knowing that it is God who judges and that the elect—those God has chosen and Jesus died for—are justified before the Lord. We are the same people Jesus will one day present as pure and undefiled to His Father (Eph. 5:27). So none of the charges leveled against us before God can stick.

As Leon Morris explains, "The believer might well be concerned about his sins and wonder whether in the end they might prevail against him. Paul is sure that they will not. Since it is God who justifies, the believer's justification can never be overthrown."[15]

What incredible news! Your standing before the Lord cannot be overthrown. Not by Satan, the accuser, and not by your own heart.

15. Morris, *Epistle to the Romans*, 337.

If God is for you, who can be against you?

REFLECT

1. Have you ever felt charged with something, either by Satan or your own heart? What was it?

2. Why is it important to remember that we have an accuser (Satan)?

3. Have you experienced the kind of false guilt or worldly sorrow described above? How can you tell the difference between this and true godly grief?

4. How does a right view of sin and a right view of guilt actually lead to freedom and grace?

5. Do you believe strongly that your justification can't be overthrown, or do you sometimes believe you are hanging on by a thread? What might you pray right now to help you believe God's Word?

WEEK SIX | DAY FOUR

EXPLORE

Who Is to Condemn?

Who is to condemn? Christ Jesus is the one who died—more than that, who was raised—who is at the right hand of God, who indeed is interceding for us.
ROMANS 8:34

My mom used to say often that she felt like a "broken record." She was referring to the old vinyl recordings, of course. If a vinyl disk is scratched or broken, the needle will skip and repeat the last thing it played over and over again. Mom felt like that when she had to remind us over and over about what we needed to do or bring, only to have us forget what she said—or (let's be honest) ignore it.

Today, as a parent, I can see exactly how my mom felt. I will tell my children something, and five minutes later I'll have to tell them again. I don't (usually) get angry that I must repeat myself often, but I do get frustrated and find myself thinking, *Don't you understand yet? Aren't you listening?*

I'm thankful that the Lord is not like me and that He is pure and patient. And yet I wonder if Paul was thinking "Don't you get it yet?" when he wrote this verse—because it brings Romans 8 full circle with yet another reassurance that no one can condemn us if we are in Christ. When a word is repeated in Scripture, we pay attention. There is a reason why we needed to be reminded yet again that there is no condemnation for those in Christ Jesus. Perhaps it's because it's safe to say that like children we will forget, even two minutes after we are told. Our hearts will attempt to condemn us every time we sin. But as 1 John 3:20–21 reminds us, "Whenever our heart condemns us, God is greater than our heart, and he knows everything. Beloved, if our heart does not condemn us, we have confidence before God."

Paul's answer to his own question—"Who is to condemn"— is also worth repeating over and over and over again. Why don't we need to worry about being condemned? Because "Christ Jesus is the one who died—more than that, who was raised—who is at the right hand of God, who indeed is interceding for us" (8:34).

Jesus died for our sins, satisfying the wrath of God; therefore, no one can condemn us.

Jesus defeated death and is at the most powerful position in the universe, at the right hand of God; therefore, no one can condemn us.

And the risen Savior is not sitting idly by. He is interceding right now for you and for me. Jesus lives to make intercession on our behalf (Heb. 7:25). The whole gospel, the good news, assures us that no one can condemn us.

At the end of your days, do you want to rely on your heart or on Jesus? Do you want to rely on your personal track record or on God's grace? It's a truth we can rest in: no one can condemn us because our Redeemer lives.

REFLECT

1. Have you ever struggled with a sense of condemnation? Why is it such a serious offense or problem before the Lord?

2. Ultimately, when we feel condemned, we are forgetting the gospel. What are some ways you can remind yourself of the gospel daily?

3. Why is Jesus' resurrection so crucial to the message of this chapter and to our faith?

4. Why is Jesus' position in heaven—seated at the right hand of God, right next to His Father—significant?

5. Notice that Romans 8 says that both the Spirit (vv. 26–27) and Jesus (v. 34) intercede on our behalf. In what ways are these intercessions alike? Different? What is your response to knowing that *both* the Holy Spirit and the Son of God are actively involved in connecting you with the Father?

WEEK SIX | DAY FIVE

EXPLORE

Who Shall Separate Us?

Who shall separate us from the love of Christ? Shall tribulation, or distress, or persecution, or famine, or nakedness, or danger, or sword? As it is written,

> "For your sake we are being killed all the day long;
> we are regarded as sheep to be slaughtered."

No, in all these things we are more than conquerors through him who loved us. For I am sure that neither death nor life, nor angels nor rulers, nor things present nor things to come, nor powers, nor height nor depth, nor anything else in all creation, will be able to separate us from the love of God in Christ Jesus our Lord.
ROMANS 8:35–39

Close your eyes and picture it. You're at the starting lineup of your local 5K road race. You have a headband on to block the sweat that will inevitably run down your face and into your eyes. You're anxiously waiting for the announcer to tell you and the hundred other participants to go. And then you remember your T-shirt. On the back of your breathable, sweat resistant tee are big bold letters: We Are More Than Conquerors! You are ready to go out and do your personal best.

But is that what Romans 8 is really all about?

Do we really want to see this triumphant and reassuring last section of Romans 8 minimized to a T-shirt slogan? Do we really want to apply these awesome words, filled with incredible and eternal truth, to just getting through our day or our road race?

Don't get me wrong. God surely cares about the mundane and ordinary things. He cares about everything we do and say and is intimately involved in our lives. But these verses aren't really about road races. They are about much more!

Here we are at Paul's fifth and final rhetorical question—really a series of questions—the culmination of the life-giving encouragement in chapter 8. And now for the first time we see that it's all about love: "the love of God in Christ Jesus." Everything that we have been learning has been wrapped up in this divine love. Every act of God is motivated by His love for us. God's love is the surety of His staying power—His love is everlasting.

But there are times when we doubt God's love for us. So Paul asks a series of pointed questions to assure us just how faithful this love is. Can any of these things separate us from the love of Christ?

- *Tribulation or distress or persecution?* Jesus says to us, "I have said these things to you, that in me you may have peace. In the world you will have tribulation. But take heart; I have overcome the world" (John 16:33). In our troubles and trials, we can have peace because we know that God is with us. We know that He is *for* us and that Jesus gives us His peace.

- *Famine or nakedness?* Jesus says, "If God so clothes the grass of the field, which today is alive and tomorrow is thrown into the oven, will he not much more clothe you . . . ?" (Matt. 6:30). God provides for all our needs. He doesn't promise us riches, but He does promise to take care of us. Neither famine nor poverty can separate us from the love of Christ.

- *Danger or sword?* A martyr might ask before dying, "Where are you, Lord?" But the Lord will surely answer, "Right here." Jesus tells of His everlasting love through danger or sword:

> Do not fear those who kill the body but cannot kill the soul. Rather fear him who can destroy both soul and body in hell. Are not two sparrows sold for a penny? And not one of them will fall to the ground apart from your Father. But even the hairs of your head are all numbered. Fear not, therefore; you are of more value than many sparrows. So everyone who acknowledges me before men, I also will acknowledge before my Father who is in heaven, but whoever denies me before men, I also will deny before my Father who is in heaven. (Matt. 10:28–33)

It is in answering these questions with Jesus' own words that we come to fully understand the victory cry, "We are more than conquerors." How are we conquerors? "Through him who loved us" (v. 37). We are not conquerors because of our will to succeed. We are not conquerors because of our strength. We are not even conquerors because we have faith. We are conquerors because of God's love for us.

In these last two culminating sentences of Romans 8, Paul emphasizes his conviction, based on the nature and character of God, that nothing—absolutely nothing!—can cut us off from the love of God in Christ Jesus. All our challenges in life—and all the good things, too—have a single purpose: to draw us near to the God who is for us. Not one thing we might think could separate us from God will be able to. And that is the essence of our victory. We are victorious in Christ Jesus and in His love, which is "steadfast, faithful and persevering."[16]

As chapter 8 comes to a close, we leave with this assurance of our faith. John Stott in his study of Romans sums this up well:

> Insecurity is written across all human experience. Christian people are not guaranteed immunity to temptation, tribulation or tragedy, but we are

---

16. John Stott, *The Message of Romans: God's Good News for the World,* The Bible Speaks Today (Book 106), (Downers Grove, IL: InterVarsity Press, 2001), 259.

promised victory over them. God's pledge is not that suffering will never afflict us, but that it will never separate us from his love.[17]

His love will never fail, will never let go, and will never allow us to be trampled. God will be faithful to us to the very end of time. With confidence and great assurance of faith, we can proclaim from the mountaintops: God is *for* us!

REFLECT

1. How have you interpreted the phrase "we are more than conquerors" in the past? In what ways (if any) has this study changed your understanding?

2. Why do you think Paul lists suffering in this list of things that can't separate us instead of sin?

3. Paul ends this incredible section of Romans 8 on the love of Christ. Why?

4. Where else in Scripture do we see a focus on the love of Jesus? Use a concordance (or other Bible study aid) to search the Scriptures, and write down any texts that directly mention the love of Jesus—as many as you can. Then take note of what is surrounding those texts (the scene, other text, what the writer is addressing). What did you learn about Jesus' love from this brief study?

17. Ibid.

5. How does Jesus' love secure our victory?

6. Have you ever felt insecure in your relationship with God? In what ways?

7. In what ways (if any) do these verses build your assurance in the faith?

8. Sum it all up. Why can we say with confidence that God is for us?

CONCLUSION

TAKE IT TO THE WORLD

I love giving my husband gifts. I daydream about what might encourage him the most. I plot about ways to sneakily purchase it. And then the anticipation of giving my gift to him just about causes me to explode. The whole process is so fun for me.

For me, writing this study of Romans 8 has been like that. This amazing chapter in Romans is like a gift from the Lord wrapped up in words of assurance and power, something I just can't keep to myself. Having completed the study, I hope you feel that way too. I hope what you have learned and studied here will motivate you to share the gospel with those who need to hear it.

The book of Romans, remember, was written to Christians, and its promises do not necessarily apply to everyone walking this earth. In other words, right now there are people who cannot proclaim, as we can, that "there is no condemnation" for us. In fact, those who do not know Jesus *do* stand condemned—and we need to take that very seriously.

One way the Lord distinguishes among people—and I'd argue this is the most important differentiation—is whether we are in Christ or not in Christ. And this distinction has eternal consequences because, as C. S. Lewis wrote in *The Weight of Glory*, we are all immortal beings:

You have never talked to a mere mortal. Nations, cultures, arts, civilisations—these are mortal, and their life is to ours as the life of a gnat. But it is immortals whom we joke with, work with, marry, snub and exploit—immortal horrors or everlasting splendours.[18]

Every human being on earth was made in the image of God. Each one has an eternal destiny—either heaven or hell. That means there is no one walking the earth who is not in need of the gospel. Eternal lives are at stake here. Hearts are at stake as well. The only way for a heart to be aflame for God is through the pursuing, saving grace of God, which transforms hearts of stone to hearts of flesh (Ezek. 36:26). And while God can and does access hearts directly, He typically chooses to do this work through humans who have tasted His love and are willing to share it.

My own testimony comes to mind here. God sent a young girl who was in love with Jesus and His gospel to share the good news with me. At that point I was not running after God—quite the opposite was true. My salvation required His pursuit. I remember this when I read Ephesians 2, and the truth of the words seems to jump off the page. I was dead, but God made me alive through Jesus' death on the cross. By a free gift, I was made alive by grace through faith (Eph. 2:1–10). I could never have saved myself—I didn't think my heart *needed* transformation—but God knew what I needed. His grace made it all possible. But—and this is crucial—He used a sinner saved by that same grace to teach me about Him.

Why in the world would I be sharing all this right now after all that good news in Romans 8? Because I've noticed a habit among my fellow believers. All too often, it seems, we will do Bible studies and learn about good things and even have our hearts and lives transformed, but we never get around to taking this good news to the world.

Jesus told His disciples to go and make disciples of all nations and to teach them (Matt. 28:19–20). We Christians have information that needs to be out in the world—information about Jesus, about what we have learned in Romans 8. But relatively few of us actually get brave and share the good news.

18. C. S. Lewis, *The Weight of Glory* (New York: HarperCollins, 2001, orig. pub. 1949), 47.

According to a LifeWay Research study conducted in 2012,[19] 80 percent of American Protestants who attend church one or more times a month believe they have a responsibility to share their faith. Of that same group, however, 61 percent had not shared the gospel in the six months prior to the study, and 48 percent had not invited an unchurched person to attend a church service or a program at their church.

Most of us are probably not surprised by these statistics, but we should be. No, they are not the ultimate guide for how we order our lives as Christians, but they suggest that we have work to do. Knowing that we have the greatest news on earth should motivate us to get up and share, invite, and engage those who might not know Jesus.

I'm not trying to guilt you here. I, too, can struggle with evangelism. But I think that if we really believe what we claim to believe, then not sharing it is a dreadful thing.

Why do we hesitate to do it? One reason is that evangelism seems complicated. But the real complication, for most of us, is in our own minds. We overthink what we need to do. We fear forgetting something or getting the message wrong. We worry about looking stupid and wonder if we even know what we're talking about. We end up not doing anything at all.

Our concern is not just with finding the right words to say—though that's not easy. (Trust me. I've been there.) The when and where and how of evangelism seems to stump people as much as, if not more than, what to actually say. Perhaps we want an angel to appear and tell us that now is the time. And of course it would be much easier if someone simply walked up to us and asked, "How do I become a Christian?" That does happen, but not often.

So how do we get around all that in order to share the good news? How can we simplify evangelism? One of the best ways I've found is to make it a part of my everyday life, and one place it can begin is the home. Hospitality is not only a

19. "Churchgoers Believe in Sharing Faith, Most Never Do," LifeWay Research, August 12, 2012, https://lifewayresearch.com/2012/08/13/churchgoers-believe-in-sharing-faith-most-never-do/.

wonderful means of sharing Christ's love in a practical way, it also provides an opportunity to build friendships and share the gospel.

To be clear, showing Christ's love to others by inviting them into our lives and homes is really important, but it is not evangelism. Sharing the gospel means we must open our mouths and actually use words, because "faith comes from hearing, and hearing through the word of Christ" (Rom. 10:17). But hospitality can definitely be one means to that end. It's a great way to set the stage for evangelism.

Hebrews 13:2 gives us a beautiful picture of hospitality: "Do not neglect to show hospitality to strangers, for thereby some have entertained angels unaware." Though this passage and others like Romans 12:13 most likely refer to caring for the needs of fellow believers, there is no doubt that the call to be hospitable applies beyond our Christian circles and church walls.

The early Christians were hospitable to those traveling—and there's no evidence that all those travelers were followers of Jesus. And even in the South where I live, where it's easy to assume that everyone is a Christian, that is not the case. All around me are people who need to hear the gospel—yes, even in the suburbs of middle Tennessee.

Opportunities to share the gospel are all around us. We have a treasure—a great treasure. We keep it in "jars of clay" (2 Cor. 4:7), which means we're human and won't get it right 100 percent of the time. But we don't have to! God is the one who does the heart work. We simply need to be faithful to share.

So I challenge you, now that you have finished Romans 8, to try reaching out to the people around you—your neighbors, people you meet at work or the park or the coffee shop, friends of friends, the parents of your kids' friends, or whoever else might enjoy a friend and a meal. While you're at it, watch for opportunities to share the hope you have found in the gospel. Keep in mind that these people are not projects or goals, but human beings like yourself made in God's image, and that you have the best news for them they could ever hear. So, out of love, share the gospel with boldness, entrusting the rest to God.

RESOURCES FOR FURTHER STUDY

The books and online resources listed below have been valuable to me as I prepared this study, and I believe they will assist you as well in your ongoing study of the book of Romans. That's right! I hope you will take your study beyond Romans 8 and dig into the entire book. It's definitely worth your while!

DeYoung, Kevin. *Taking God at His Word: Why the Bible Is Knowable, Necessary, and Enough, and What That Means for You and Me.* Wheaton, IL: Crossway, 2014.

Grudem, Wayne, gen. ed. *ESV Study Bible.* Wheaton, IL: Crossway, 2008.

Keller, Timothy. *Romans 8–16 for You.* London, UK: Good Book Company, 2014.

Kruger, Michael J. *Canon Revisited: Establishing the Origins and Authority of the New Testament Books.* Wheaton, IL: Crossway, 2012.

———— *Romans Bible Study.* Season 1 (Romans 1–7). Charlotte, NC: Reformed Theological Seminary, 2014. Video series. https://www.rts.edu/Site/RTSNearYou/Charlotte/rbs1.aspx.

———— *Romans Bible Study.* Season 2 (Romans 8–16). Charlotte, NC: Reformed Theological Seminary, 2014. Video series. http://rts.edu/Site/RTSNearYou/Charlotte/rbs2.aspx.

Moo, Douglas J. *The Epistle of the Romans.* The International Commentary on the New Testament. Grand Rapids, MI: Eerdmans, 1996.

Morris, Leon. *The Epistle to the Romans.* Reprint edition. Grand Rapids, MI: Eerdmans, 2012, orig. pub. 1988.

Stott, John. *The Message of Romans: God's Good News for the World.* The Bible Speaks Today (Book 106). Downers Grove, IL: InterVarsity, 2001.

Thomas, Derek W. H. *How the Gospel Brings Us All the Way Home.* Lake Mary, FL: Reformation Trust, 2011.

We will never be short on fears.

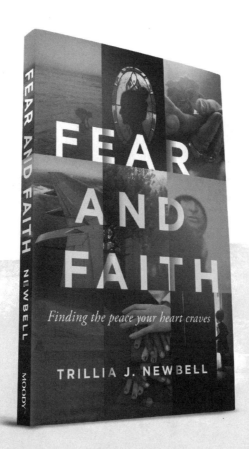

The fears we carry can paralyze our spirit, damage our relationships, and hinder our faith. *Fear and Faith* is a meditation upon God's trustworthiness. By sharing reflections on Scripture, her own experiences, and the stories of other women, Trillia Newbell shows you a God big enough to replace your fears with faith.

978-0-8024-1022-1 | also available as an eBook

MOODY
Publishers®

From the Word to Life®

What's the view from where you worship?

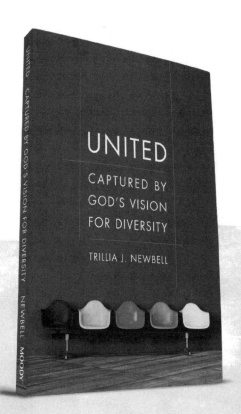

United will inspire, challenge, and encourage readers to pursue the joys of diversity through stories of the author's own journey and a theology of diversity lived out. In the pages of *United*, Trillia Newbell reveals the deeply moving, transforming power of knowing—really knowing—someone who is equal yet unique.

978-0-8024-1014-6 | also available as an eBook

MOODY
Publishers®

*From the Word **to** Life*®